CROCHET FOR BEGINNERS THE BIBLE

10 in 1

The Step-by-Step Crash Course for Beginners to Master the Art of Crochet, Learn Essential Techniques, and Create Stunning Projects | Ignite Your Crochet Journey Today

Lisa Jones

Contents

Introduction

Greetings from the amazing world of crochet! For many years, crochet has captivated the hearts and minds of craft enthusiasts due to its versatility and age. This ebook is your key to unleashing the creative possibilities of crochet, regardless of your level of experience. It is ideal for both novice and seasoned crocheters wishing to improve.

You'll learn how to work magic with a ball of yarn to create lovely, useful, and artistic objects in the pages that follow. Crochet provides countless opportunities for creativity and self-expression, from soft blankets and fashionable garments to elaborate lace doilies and cute amigurumi.

This e-book serves as your all-in-one crochet handbook, covering everything from basic knowledge about yarn and hooks to more complex methods and designs. We'll guide you through the projects, designs, and stitches that will enable you to become an expert in this age-old trade.

Crochet has several uses, including making unique gifts, embellishing your house, and providing a creative hobby or way to decompress. Now that you have your yarn and hooks, let's explore the world of crocheting. We'll solve the puzzles piece by piece and assist you in crafting lovely, one-of-a-kind items that you, your family, and your house will treasure. Crochet is ready to inspire you whether you're searching for a new pastime or a love that will last a lifetime. Together, let's embark on this crocheting journey!

Let's dive in for more information!

1: CROCHET FOR BEGINNERS

Chapter 1
Crochet Fundamentals

Crochet is a wonderful form of needlecraft that allows you to create beautiful fabric by using a hook to work with loops of yarn. Crochet is a versatile craft that allows you to create a wide range of items, including blankets, scarves, hats, and sweaters. If you are searching for an enjoyable and imaginative way to utilize your spare time, crochet might just be the ideal activity for you!

This section has all the information you need to get started. If you are new to crocheting, use these pages to acquaint yourself with terminology and basic concepts. Even if you are a seasoned crocheter, you can still often refer to this section for guidance. Let us take a closer look at all aspects of it!

Why Is It Called "Crochet?"

The term crochet comes from the French word crochet, which is a small hook, derived from the Germanic word croc.   The stitch known as crocheting was utilized in 17th-century French lace-making to connect different pieces of lace together.

 The art of crochet has a rich and diverse heritage, spanning countless generations and cultures.   The name probably developed from the French term because of the widespread prominence and influence of French style and civilization in the world of sewing.

The History of Crochet

Various cultures have asserted their rich crochet history, hailing from countries such as the nation of France, The southern part of Africa, England, Italy, Arabia, along China. However, the true origin of crochet still remains a mystery.   According to some fiber artists, crochet is said to have originated in the Middle East and quickly spread to Spain, similar to the way knitting did.

However, it is widely believed by historians that the craft has its origins in the Far East, eventually gaining popularity in the Western world during the early 1800s. Having its origins shrouded in mystery, the art of crochet has quickly gained popularity and made a significant global impact.   What was once a vital skill for survival, crocheting has evolved into a beautiful art form!

In 1829, Mademoiselle Riego de la Branchardiere penned the very first crochet pattern. With a French father as well as an Irish mother, she has earned the title of the pioneer of crochet and is credited with originating the renowned Irish crochet style!   At the age of 18, she successfully published her debut book on the subject of fiber and needlework.

These patterns have a beautiful and intricate design, perfect for special occasions rather than everyday use.   The intricate designs of these pieces showcase the maker's exceptional skill and attention to detail.   Mademoiselle Riego released a book on knitting along with crochet trends in 1846.

Queen Victoria played a significant role in the history of crochet. She had a preference for Irish crochet and opted to buy it instead of pricier, more delicate lace. After the passing of her husband Albert, Victoria took up crocheting and in 1900, she skillfully crafted eight scarves that were presented to veterans of the Boer war. The scarves were proudly received and worn as sashes by those who received them. Crochet has remained a beloved craft, capturing the interest and admiration of people for decades.

Today, crochet has evolved beyond intricate doily designs and shawls. Crochet has gained immense popularity as a hobby and is even utilized in therapy to effectively alleviate stress and anxiety! If you are intrigued by the idea of becoming part of the worldwide community of crocheters, we offer a selection of starter kits to assist you in embarking on your latest hobby!

How to Get Started with Crochet?

Are you prepared to begin? Continue reading to acquire the fundamentals of crocheting so that, armed with these clear-cut, beginner-friendly crochet instructions, you may confidently begin your first project.

I love crocheting as a pastime. It is lightweight, reasonably priced, requires few tools, and yields aesthetically pleasing yet useful objects. Apart from that, though, I think crocheting is capable of many more than just creating lovely objects!

We'll cover all you need to know to start crocheting, including basic stitches, how to hold the hook and yarn, and where to look for your first projects, in this detailed bible.

Crocheting can be quite challenging. Hours are spent deciphering patterns and attempting freestyle crochet. Mistakes are made, projects are unraveled, and the process starts anew. The final crochet piece often differs from the original vision, presenting a multitude of obstacles to overcome. Rest assured, this book is designed to assist you with various aspects

- Discover various crochet techniques
- Understand crochet terminology and can decipher patterns.

- It is important to have a solid understanding of crochet instructions in order to effectively navigate crochet patterns.

- Learn the fundamentals of crochet stitches
- Master the art of crochet for both left-handed and right-handed individuals
- Learn about common mistakes in crochet and discover effective ways to prevent and fix them.

And many more so stay tuned!

Essential Crochet Tools Every Beginner Should Have?

Yarn is essential for any crochet project, making it a top priority for beginners. Selecting yarn is an exciting aspect of beginning a new project. Personally, we can spend hours simply selecting stunning color combinations. However, when you are embarking on your first crochet project and come across shelves filled with a wide variety of yarn options, your initial excitement might turn into a sense of unease.

You cannot create any crochet projects without it. ...

- Crochet hooks
- Scissors
- Stitch markers
- Tapestry needle
- Row counter
- Blocking mats
- Looking for needle threads

However, things can be simpler if you have access to more tools. You'll have whatever you need to get began on your crochet voyage when you have these basic crochet supplies with you.

Chapter 2
Choosing Your Crochet Supplies, Materials Accessories

Knitting and crocheting have the advantage of not requiring a lot of intricate instruments and supplies to store or transport. This art form is quite portable!

One of the most thrilling aspects of pursuing a new interest is uncovering the multitude of enjoyable tools at your disposal! In this section on crocheting accessories, you will discover everything you need to create a wide range of projects, from simple to intricate designs.

I will provide you with a comprehensive list of crochet accessories, including tips on where to save money and where to indulge in your crafting pursuits. Here, I will be sharing all of my experiences with crochet accessories.

This section aims to assist those who are new to crochet or have some experience but still consider themselves beginners. It provides guidance and support for their crochet journey. Seasoned professionals may consider it somewhat ambiguous, but stay tuned to see if there is something valuable you can glean from it. Allow me to provide you with more in-depth information so that you can make an informed decision.

Selecting the Perfect Yarn

Many knitters and crocheters express their love for their craft by highlighting the wide range of yarn options available, with their diverse textures and vibrant colors. I am absolutely passionate about it.

In most cases, projects that call for bulky yarns will need bigger hooks. For projects worked with very fine yarn, it is important to use a smaller hook. Crochet patterns typically provide suggestions for the type and weight of yarn, as well as the recommended hook size. You have the option to replace the yarn, as long as you make sure to check your gauge.

There is an extensive selection of yarn for crocheters to choose from. Alongside traditional materials like cotton and wool, linen, silk, as well as acrylics, you will find options such as bamboo, wheat, and sugar cane fibers. Any type of yarn can be used for crocheting, although certain yarns may present more challenges during the process. When working with highly textured yarns like ribbon, eyelashes, lumps and bobbles, it can be a bit challenging to see the stitches. However, the end results can be absolutely stunning.

Understanding Types of Yarn

Knitting yarns are made of various materials and fibers, each with special properties of their own. Both natural and synthetic fibers are available; they differ in cost, feel, and utility.

Natural yarn fibers, like wool, cotton, and silk, are derived from plants or animals, as their name implies. Man-made synthetic fibers include polyester and acrylic. The majority of producers combine synthetic and natural fibers to produce yarns that have particular desired qualities, such as softness.

Here are a few sorts of yarn fibers.

- The wool comes in a variety of types, including lamb's wool, merino, pure new wool/virgin synthetic Icelandic wool, and washable wool.
- Soft and luxurious materials like mohair and cashmere
- Materials such as nylon, acrylic, rayon, and polyester
- Fabrics such as silk, cotton, linen, and rayon
- Unique yarns create distinct patterns in knitted pieces, such as tweed, heather, marled (ragg), and variegated
- Crochet thread - specifically crafted for the art of crocheting. Offered in a variety of weights, thicknesses, twists, and finishes. Typically, crochet threads are crafted from pure cotton fiber. Crochet thread is comparable to yarn, with the fiber becoming thinner as the thread number increases. Common sizes include 3 and 10, suitable for a variety of uses such as tablecloths, table runners, doilies, and bedspreads. It is important to use the correct hook size for your threads, as specified on the product label or a pattern.
- Unique materials such as ribbon, boucle, chenille, thick-thin, railroad ribbon, and faux fur, among others.

Picking the Right Crochet Hook

Crochet hooks can be divided into two main categories, and many crochet enthusiasts have favored one type over the other. Often, their preference is as straightforward as enjoying the type of hook you utilized when you first learned to crochet.

Inline hooks

Inline hooks typically feature pointed heads that are equal in size to their shorter shafts. Many crocheters believe that using an inline hook can result in stitches of the same size and help maintain a steady tension.

Tapered hooks

Tapered hooks typically feature a rounded head, a smaller throat compared to the shaft, and a longer shaft length. Some crocheters prefer the added length for improved mobility when maneuvering their stitches.

It ultimately boils down to your individual taste. There are numerous techniques for gripping your crochet hook. The method you select will vary depending on the kind of crochet task you are working on and what feels most comfortable for you.

There are typically two main grips that most people choose from:

- The Pencil Grip You hold your hook in a way that resembles how you would hold a pencil, using a three-fingered pinch.
- The Knife Grip You hold your hook in a firm grip, with your last three fingers guiding its movement.

Crochet Thread Selection

A thinner substitute for ordinary yarn is crochet thread. The majority of it is composed of cotton or cotton blends; acrylic may also be used in some cases. Numerous tasks, like as tablecloths, doilies, and items like hats and scarves, can be made with it.

There is a wide range of sizes available for crochet thread, ranging from 3 to 100. Some of these sizes can resemble traditional yarn, while others are more similar to sewing thread. It is important to keep in mind that the thickness of crochet thread increases as the number decreases. In contrast to traditional yarn sizing, the size of the yarn increases as the number goes up. As an illustration, size 20 appears significantly slimmer compared to size 3 or 10. It may take some time to adjust, but once you become familiar with it, you will be fine.

There are several popular thread sizes available, including 3, 5, 10, 20, and 30. The dimensions 3 and 5 crochet thread can have a similar thickness to a lightweight yarn. Starting with a crochet thread can be a breeze, especially when you are transitioning from other projects. Consider reserving sizes 20 or 30 for when you have refined your crochet thread skills.

Thread sizes are generally consistent across different brands, with the exception of Pearl thread. This thread utilizes a distinct numbering system. The thread has a soft, glossy texture that resembles silk. We offer this type of thread in sizes 3, 5, and 8. If a pattern requires pearl thread, it is important to use this specific type in order to achieve the desired size for the final product.

The Importance of Dye Lot

For hobby knitters and crocheters, the dye lot number is crucial information because using yarn that comes from various dye lots can detract from the handmade textiles' aesthetic appeal. Make sure you get all the yarn you'll need for a project at once because the finished item may reveal subtle differences in shading between different dye lots.

Make sure the washing instructions are identical for any yarn varieties you are combining in a single project. The product label contains care recommendations; carefully follow these directions for optimal results. Furthermore, always remember to create a swatch in order to measure the gauge; more on that later.

Other equipments:

The equipment and materials needed for crochet are minimal and straightforward. In addition to essential tools like a hook, yarn, as well as scissors, there are some other optional items that can be useful.

- A yarn needle is typically crafted from either plastic or metal and features a blunt point and a generously sized eye. It is commonly utilized to neatly conceal loose ends when connecting yarn or completing a project.

- Scissors: It is recommended to use a small pair of blunt-end scissors that are in good condition.

- A tape measure is typically utilized to take body metrics or to measure the length and width of a project, helping you determine the necessary gauge for the pattern.

- T pins are essential tools for blocking and securing various pieces of a portrait together, whether you are joining them or taking measurements.

- Gauge ruler: An L-shaped window item that measures the number of stitches and rows in an inch, making it easy to keep track of your knitting or crochet projects.

- Split markers: Convenient round plastic spiral elements that easily slide into crochet work. They are commonly employed to mark specific points in crocheting, such as joining ongoing rounds or making increases and decreases.

- Box to store the items mentioned above: Containers such as a pencil container, eyeglass case, or trip toothbrush holder can be useful for organizing hooks, scissors, as well as yarn needles. A film container is perfect for storing split markers.

- Folder and possibly notebook: This will assist in organizing and storing handouts. You

- will always have a reliable source of valuable information when it has a designated place.

Chapter 3
Deciphering Crochet Patterns

Reading written crochet patterns can feel like reading a foreign language when you're initially learning the craft but you'll be stitching away in no time if you get the terminology. To begin, all you'll need to know is a few popular crochet terminology and symbols, along with a few fundamental stitch abbreviations. Additionally, you must be able to comprehend the specifications for your pattern, including the gauge, type of yarn, and necessary tools.

Reading a Crochet Pattern

Here's a simple overview of the most crucial information regarding crochet pattern reading, starting from the very start:

After selecting your pattern, take some time to review it and make sure you understand all the requirements for the project. The following sections are found in most crochet patterns:

- A section under "about" with pattern notes
- Yarn, supplies, and ideas required
- Specifics regarding gauge, tension, and/or size
- Use of abbreviations
- Any unique stitching applied

All of these offer helpful information that is frequently essential to know before starting. Let's examine them in more detail.

A lot of crochet designs are organized by level of skill. Before picking out a new design, make sure you carefully read the packet to see what level of skill it is meant for. If you have never done this before, start with designs that are made for beginners. If you can read these levels of crochet patterns well, you can move on to reading intermediate and advanced levels.

Also, keep an eye out for patterns that come with how-to videos. Some will take you to

YouTube instructional clips, while others come with step-by-step picture guides that are very helpful in addition to the crochet pattern. Finally, you have found the right pattern for your level of skill. It is time to get to know the pattern or kit you are using. Take some time to look through every significant detail before you start looking at the pattern. Go through everything in detail, and if necessary, take notes.

Tips for Successful Pattern Reading

The following advice can help you read patterns successfully:

- Learn the following terminology and abbreviations: Numerous acronyms and words are used in crochet patterns, which reduce space consumption and improve readability. Certain abbreviations, like fundamental stitch abbreviations, are simple to comprehend. Online resources provide a comprehensive glossary of crochet words and abbreviations along with definitions.

- Keep an eye out for symbols: crochet patterns include a number of symbols to instruct you on what to do in addition to a plethora of acronyms and terminology. For instance, parenthesis () is frequently used to define a group of threads that should be worked together, while asterisks (*) are used to signify repeats.

- Examine the pattern closely: Make sure that you comprehend all the language and acronyms by reading the printed pattern from beginning to end before beginning. Before beginning to work on any row, read through all of the crochet instructions once you have a clear idea of what you will be doing overall.

- Practice: It is a good idea to go through a few rounds using the yarn or thread and crochet hook you plan to use before beginning a pattern. You may quickly identify any issues with the design or your comprehension of it by testing a portion of it first.

- Take notes: As you work, jot down notes on the design and cross out the rows that you finish. This will assist you in tracking your position within the pattern and help you stay clear of errors.

- Verify and confirm again: Before you begin crocheting, be sure you understand every step of the process. It is very simple to get overly excited about a project and jump right in without knowing what to expect. Before you begin crocheting, be sure you know precisely what you are doing.

You may properly read and comprehend crochet designs and produce lovely products by using these tips.

Understanding Skill Levels in Crochet

Crochet design skill levels are divided into four categories.

- For novice crocheters, beginner or basic projects have fundamental crochet stitches, straightforward stitch repetitions, and little shaping.
- Simple crochet stitches with basic variations are used in easy crafts. These jobs could involve basic shape, finishing, and color changes.
- A wide range of crochet stitches and methods, as well as intermediate shaping and finishing skills, will be used in intermediate projects.
- Complex or experienced crochet projects will feature complicated and varied patterns, non-repeating color changes, and expertly shaped and finished edges.

Chapter 4
Exploring Crochet Patterns

There are two different types of crochet patterns: written and charted. Patterns are composed of words and abbreviations that explain the stitches as well as techniques employed in the design. Charted patterns utilize symbols to depict the stitches along with techniques employed in the pattern. This stitch diagram contains all the necessary information to help you create the project.

- Written instructions are perfect for beginners as they offer in-depth guidance on every stitch and technique.
- Charted patterns are ideal for individuals who prefer visual aids, as they provide a clear representation of the pattern in graph form.

Written Crochet Pattern

There are certain common elements that can be found in well-written crochet patterns. Every section about the pattern contains valuable information that should not be overlooked. There are a minimum of 9 sections included in the pattern:

- Pattern Name and Author
- List of Materials including yarn type, amount, and color
- Gauge Information
- Size of Finished Product
- Difficulty Level
- Abbreviations and/or Symbols Used
- Special Stitches, if necessary
- Additional Notes
- Step-by-Step Instructions

How do I read a crochet chart and what is it?

What are known as crochet charts or crochet diagrams are used by some pattern makers. Furthermore, these diagrams may appear to novices to be written in an antiquated language. However, they don't have to be overly intricate, particularly when working in the round. Locating the first stitch is the first step. It sits in the middle of the diagram while working in rounds. After that, you'll proceed outside.

A chain is typically denoted with a flat oval, while a slip stitch is typically indicated with a dot. An x or a + sign can be made out of a single crochet. A T designates half-double crochet stitches. Treble crochet stitches have two crossbeams, whereas double crochet stitches have a T with one.

In every letter line, the single crochet crochet stitches form a V with a single crossbeam. It's the same as the single crochet reduction but reversed. In half-double crochet, the crossbeam goes to the top of the V's lines when working up and down. Crossbeams are placed at the top and in the middle of the lines in double crochet rises and reductions.

It is a good idea to stick with designs when you are first learning to crochet. rather than charts. They make it simpler to read and monitor your stitches. As you become more proficient, you might encounter a pattern in a language you are unfamiliar with, in which case a chart might be necessary. Thus, knowing the symbols can still be useful to you later on.

You now possess the necessary equipment to begin your new pastime. Crocheting may seem intimidating at first, but it is not as hard as you might think once you understand a little of the terminology.

Eventually, those symbols and abbreviations that used to cause you so much difficulty will become instantly familiar to you. If you are new to crocheting, watching movies that break down the patterns could be useful. That is where The Woobles come in. You will not ever have to worry about not grasping the pattern because the Woobles novice kits will guide you through every round.

Meanings of Symbols in Crochet Patterns

Crochet patterns utilize symbols to represent various stitches and methods in addition to abbreviations. These symbols are typically seen in the legend or pattern key. Typical symbols found in patterns for crocheting include the following:

YO: yarn over

*: repeat

(): task instructions enclosed in parenthesis, repeated as needed

[]: follow the task instructions enclosed in parentheses as often as necessary

-: work instructions among hyphens as frequently as specified

It's important to comprehend crochet symbols because they make it easier to follow the pattern. Consult the legend or pattern key if you are unclear about the meaning of any symbol.

Chapter 5
Mastering Basic Crochet Stitches

We'll discuss the fundamental crochet stitches that any novice should be familiar with in this part. They're not too hard, and if you master them, reading new patterns and creating more crochet products won't be too difficult for you!

You will learn all the basic crochet stitches and everything you need to understand about crocheting from this, including:

Single Crochet Stitch

It's a quick simple stitch with multiple versions. Several patterns, including all amigurumi crochet work, employ this stitch a lot.

Steps

- Yarn over and pull up a loop after inserting the hook into the work (the second chain from the hook on the starting chain).
- Pull the yarn through each loop on the hook and re-knit.
- Made one SC. Hook into the following stitch; continue from * in step 1.

Double Crochet Stitch

A higher stitch than half double crochet and single crochet is utilized in more complex crocheting techniques such as filet crochet, v-stitch crochet, granny squares, and numerous other well-known designs with numerous variations.

Steps

- Wrap the yarn within the hook from back to front, known as yarn over (yo).
- Place the hook into the third place chain from the hook (or as indicated in the pattern).

- Wrap the yarn around and gently pull up a loop (you should have three cycles on the hook).
- Loop the yarn over once more and gently pull it through the first pair of loops on the hook, leaving two loops remaining.

Chain Stitch

Chain stitches, the most fundamental crochet stitch, are frequently used in three distinct manners:

- Want to start a crocheting project. A beginning chain, base chain, or foundation chain is a collection of chain stitches.
- A turning chain is crocheted in between rows of stitches.
- To join each stitch in a crochet design, particularly when working in a circular.

Steps

- Start at the end of the stitch line.
- Re-insert your needle extremely near the exit point so that it emerges ahead of the stitch line.
- Pull out the thread after looping it under the needle. In the chain, you have only made one link.
- After inserting your needle within this link, exit it along the stitch line.
- To make the next link, loop the thread underneath the needle and remove it.
- Until the chain stitch reaches the required length, keep repeating the procedure.

Slip Stitch

The shortest crochet stitch is called a slip stitch. Slip patterns are not frequently used alone to create a huge piece of cloth, in contrast to other stitches. The slip stitch is used for shaping, connecting, and, if needed, transferring the yarn to a new location in the cloth in preparation for the following step. Of all the fundamental crochet stitches, the slip stitch is the simplest and mostly a method rather than a stitch.

Steps

- Hook into appropriate stitch.
- Yarn over (YO) and draw back through the loop that is on the hook as well as the st.

Half Double Crochet

The midway point between one single crochet (sc) and a double crochet (dc) is known as the half double crochet stitch (hdc). In contrast to a single (sc) stitch, this one calls for a yarn to be pulled through all three loops on the hook before the hook is inserted into the stitch.

Steps

- Create a foundation chain that is the appropriate length.
- Make another two chains. The turning chain is made up of these stitches. Yarn over the hook.
- Hook up the hook in the designated stitch.
- On your hook, there will be three loops. Again, yank over the hook.
- Again, yarn over the hook.
- Pull through the hook's three loops.
- In each stitch along the foundation chain, repeat steps 4 through 8 once more.
- To begin the next row, chain two and turn your work.

Slipknot

To secure the yarn to the crochet hook, use a slip knot of some kind. In many crochet projects, the initial step is to make a slip knot. Making it involves tying a basic loop at the yarn's end, putting the loop on the crochet hook, and drawing it taut.

Steps

- Grasp the end of the yarn with your left hand and form a loop.
- Loop the yarn over the top of the standing end.
- Secure the loop by passing it under the end of the yarn.

- Thread the loop through the hole.

- Ensure a secure knot by gently tugging on the yarn's standing end.

Simple Decrease Techniques

Mastering crochet decreases will give your fabric a beautiful shape, making them a valuable technique for creating well-fitting garments. A basic decrease in a pattern is known as dc2tog, which involves merging two double-crochet stitches into a single stitch. A greater reduction of two dc stitches is referred to as dc3tog, and so forth.

Steps: Single Crochet Decrease

- Place the hook into the first stitch.

- Wrap the yarn over and pull it through the loop.

- Finish the stitch in a different way than usual.

- Place the hook into the next stitch.

- Wrap the yarn around and pull it through the loop.

- Wrap the yarn around and then pull it through all three loops on the hook.

Steps: Half Double Crochet Decrease

- Knit one stitch.

- Place the hook into the first stitch.

- Wrap the yarn around and pull it through the loop.

- Knit one stitch.

- Place the hook into the next stitch.

- Wrap the yarn around and pull it through the loop.

- Wrap the yarn around and then pull it through all three loops on the hook.

Steps: Double Crochet Decrease

- Knit one stitch.
- Place the hook into the first stitch.
- Wrap the yarn around and pull it through the loop.
- Knit one, purl two.
- Place the hook into the next stitch.
- Wrap the yarn around and pull it through the loop.
- Wrap the yarn over and then pull it through two loops.
- Complete the stitch by pulling the yarn through the last two loops.

Decreasing is a crucial technique in crochet that allows you to shape your work and achieve a variety of patterns and designs.

Treble Crochet

Taller than a double crochet, a treble stitch (sometimes known as a triple crochet) is created by working twin yarn over at the beginning of the stitch rather than the single yarn overused in a double crochet. It's shortened to tr.

Steps

- Create a foundation chain that is the appropriate length.
- Twirl twice over the hook.
- Hook up the hook in the designated stitch Yarn over the hook.
- Insert the yarn inside the stitch. On your hook, there will be four loops of Yarn over the hook.
- Thread the yarn through the hook's two loops. On your hook, there will be three loops.
- Yarn over the hook.
- Thread the yarn through the hook's two loops. On your hook, there will be two loops of Yarn over the hook.
- Pull the yarn through the hook's final two loops.
- For every stitch along the foundation chain, repeat steps 2 through 11 once.

Easy Increase Methods

This is the method for preserving the stitch count and form of your project. To enhance the size, you add 2 or more stitches to the stitch from the prior row. 1: A single double crochet stitch is worked into the stitches below. 2: Two doubling crochet stitches are worked into the stitch below, resulting in an increase of 1. There are a few simple ways to increase a single crochet stitch, a half double crochet stitch, a double crochet stitch, and a triple crochet stitch.

Specialty Stitches: Bullion, Shell, Granny Triangle

Many crochet stitch patterns, regardless of their apparent complexity, are created by combining basic stitches. Small shifts in the stitch-ensuring procedure or changing the spot and manner of placing the hook into the fabric can produce a range of different effects.

Bullion

The roll stitch, also referred to as the bullion stitch, is a fantastic technique that adds a unique and stylish touch to crochet projects. This stitch is simply created by wrapping yarn within a crochet hook and dragging through all loops once the desired amount of wraps is achieved.

Shells and groups

Groups and shells are made up of several stitches joined together in one place. You can work them as a part of a pattern or as an increase. You can work groups and shells in half double crochets, double crochets or longer stitches.

Granny Triangle

You can work granny stitches flat in straight lines and stripes, rectangle or square granny, triangle granny (Crochet Triangle shawl), and granny square granny. Granny stitch is made up of two basic stitches: double crochet and chain stitch.

Mastering the various basic stitches is essential when it comes to learning the art of crochet. It is not necessary to learn all the staples at once. With just a few simple stitches and some beautiful yarn, you will be able to create stunning striped blankets as well as pillow covers. Learn slowly!

Chapter 6
Essential Knowledge for Beginners

Foundation Single Crochet Stitch (FSC)

A foundation single crochet, or FSC, creates two elements in one stitch by beginning with a chain and adding the single crochet thereafter. The outcome is an even more attractive first row of single crochet than you would have with a standard start.

Method

- With your crochet hook, tie a slip knot first, and then make two chains.
- Start the first chain stitch with your hook inserted.
- Pull up one loop and yank over. After completing this step, there should be a pair of loops on the hook.
- Twirl the yarn around and pass it through the hook's initial loop. It is essentially a chain stitch that you simply pull through the yarn. To ensure you do not forget, go ahead and attach a detachable stitch indicator to this chain stitch.
- To produce a single crochet, yank over and pull through both loops on your hook. When you finish this step, there should be one loop on the hook. You have successfully completed your first foundational crochet stitch.
- Do you recall how, in Step 4, you created a chain? You will now be working into that chain. Your crochet hook should be inserted into the gap created by the chain and single crochet.
- Pull up a single loop and yank over. On your hook, there need to be two loops. Pull the fiber through the initial loop on your hook once you have yanked it over. Your following chain stitch has just been completed. This is an excellent opportunity to relocate the stitch marker to the surrounding area of the chain stitch (as seen in the above photo).

- To complete the second foundational crochet stitch, pull through each loop on the hook by yarn over.
- Continue with steps 6 to 8 until the required number of stitches for your project is reached.

Give yourself a high five when you finish the first row, then turn in your work. You are prepared to proceed to the next row, whoever that may be.

Half-Double Crochet Stitch (HDC)

The midway point between a single crochet (sc) and a double crochet (dc) is known as the half dual crochet stitch (hdc). In contrast to a single (sc) stitch, this one calls for a yarn to be pulled through all three loops on the hook before the hook is inserted into the stitch.

Method

- Wrap the yarn over the needle.
- Place the hook beneath the upper loops of the following stitch.
- Make sure to yarn over.   Thread the yarn via the stitch to create a loop.
- There might be three loops on the hook.
- Make sure to yarn over.   Thread the yarn via all trio loops on the hook.   There should be a single loop remaining on the hook.

Calculating Yarn Requirements

Yards required = (length x breadth x gauge) / 6. The gauge is given in stitches per inch, while both width and length are given in inches. To translate the outcome from square inches to yards, divide the result by 6. For instance, (48 x 8 x 5) / 6 = 320 yards would be needed to make a scarf that is 48" long and 8" wide using worsted weight yarn.

Blocking Your Finished Projects

Blocking is a step you take after weaving in your ends while finishing a crochet creation. It entails wetting or dampening the fibers and then pinning them to a board so that your item may dry and take on the final shape you've imagined.

Method

Put your project in a tub of cold water and let it be there for twenty minutes to soak. Instead of wringing or twisting, carefully push out any extra water after draining the water. To assist in blotting away the remaining water, use towels. To dry, place the object flat on blocking boards.

Customizing Base Chains and Altering Colors

Adding different colors in crochet can bring a whole new level of visual appeal and depth to your projects. Here are some easy steps to change colors in crochet, whether you are performing in rows or rounds:

- Put down your crochet hook: Make sure to pause your crocheting just before you pull via the last two cycles on the crochet hook.
- Let go of the outdated hue: Let go of the outdated hue of yarn.
- Hang the new color on the hook: Place the fresh yarn color onto the hook and utilize it to draw through the final two turns on the hook.
- Keep on crocheting: Keep crocheting with the fresh shade.

There are multiple techniques to alter colors in crochet, but this simple method is applicable to various crochet stitches such as single crochet, double stitch, treble stitch, or half-double crochet.

HERE IS YOU FREE GIFT!

"The Complete Guide to the Maintenance and Care of Crocheted Artifacts"

SCAN HERE TO DOWNLOAD IT

Here's what you will find inside this fantastic guide:

1. Preserve the Beauty of Your Creation: Discover how to maintain the beauty and longevity of your crochet items with practical and detailed tips.
2. Expand Your Crafting Skills: Enhance your crochet expertise by learning the best care practices, ensuring your creations are always at their finest

2: CROCHET TIPS & TRICKS AND COMMON MISTAKES

Chapter 1
Troubleshooting Common Mistakes and how to prevent them?

If you have ever struggled with crochet and felt frustrated, this section is here to provide some guidance and help you overcome any obstacles! Here are some common crochet blunders to avoid if you are new to crocheting.

By steering clear of these errors, you will be able to improve and enhance your crocheting abilities. Clearly, as someone new to this, it is expected that you will not have everything figured out right away. But I am right here to help you avoid the typical errors that beginners often make in crocheting.

What are the common mistakes?

Here are certain common errors that can occur while crocheting:

- Making a mistake by choosing the wrong chain to start a project is a common error, especially for beginners.
- Not properly finishing the ends: Ensuring that your ends are securely woven in is crucial upon completing a project.
- Creating overly tight stitches: This issue often arises from gripping the yarn too firmly and wrapping it tightly around the hook.
- Choosing the incorrect crochet hook size: Opting for a hook that is too tiny can result in tight and challenging stitches, whereas using a hook that is too broad can lead to loose stitches and an oversized project.
- Keeping track of stitches: This can lead to an excess or shortage of stitches.

- Having trouble grasping all the crochet acronyms or terms, especially when it comes to the differences between UK and US terminology: Understanding the jargon used in crochet structures is crucial.
- Excluding the need to count stitches: Regularly counting your stitches is crucial for accurately following the pattern.
- Not understanding the pattern correctly: It can be quite tempting to dive into a new project without thoroughly reading through the pattern.
- Making a mistake when crocheting into the inappropriate part of the stitch can result in stitches that appear different.
- Feeling discouraged: As a beginner in crocheting, it is inevitable to make a few mistakes. But that is how you gain knowledge! Do not worry about being perfect; it will only make you feel like giving up.

By familiarizing yourself with these common errors, you can steer clear of them and enhance your crochet abilities.

Preventing Crochet Errors

Here are the measures to correct a crochet error:

- Spot the error: Locate the mistake in your crocheting work.
- Remove the stitches: Take care to meticulously remove the stitches until you reach the point where the error occurred.
- Correct the error: Ensure the mistake is rectified by properly redoing the stitches.
- Secure the ends: Make sure to secure the ends of the fresh yarn to keep it in place.

There are various methods to rectify a crochet error, depending on the nature of the mistake and the specific project at hand. It is crucial to approach the task with care and avoid rushing, as haste can result in further errors. Through consistent practice, you will gain greater confidence in rectifying errors and enhancing your crochet abilities.

Overcoming Challenges in Crochet

Crocheting can be quite intimidating for beginners, as it involves acquiring a new set of skills and conquering different obstacles. In addition, it requires a great deal of patience, attention to detail, and determination to accomplish a polished final product. Crochet can be challenging due to the initial learning curve involved in mastering basic stitches, comprehending patterns, and working with yarn delicately.

The world of crochet can be quite intricate, with a wide range of stitching, patterns, and strategies to explore. Nevertheless, the joy of crafting intricate layouts and tactile appearances can make the travel worthwhile. By practicing regularly, staying determined, and finding joy in the process, crocheting can become a fulfilling and captivating pastime.

To overcome these challenges, consider making small swatches using different stitches to enhance your overall technique. This can help you simulate and master a variety of stitches without the need to finish an entire project for each one. Try out various hooks and types of yarn to discover a comfortable combo to work with as you practice. Check out this article for tips on selecting the perfect crochet hook for someone new to the craft.

If you are finding it difficult, consider seeking advice from a different source. Occasionally, a fresh perspective on a stitch can be truly transformative. If you have been relying on traditional books for learning, why not explore the world of video tutorials available on platforms like YouTube?

Chapter 2
Tips for Perfecting Your Crochet Skills

Perfection Tips

Follow these tips for perfection in crocheting.

- If you are new to knitting, it is helpful to begin with larger needles and thicker yarn. This way, you will be able to clearly see the stitches as you work.

- Attach a binder clip to the edge of a bowl to conveniently secure your yarn. This will guide the working yarn and prevent the ball from rolling around. Alternatively, you can utilize a teapot and yarn the thread via the spout!

- Remember to use a clinging note to mark your spot in the pattern. It glides effortlessly!

- Stick to simple patterns if you want to showcase textured and fancy yarns. Explore more intricate cable patterns and designs using basic yarns.

- It is best to complete the row before taking a break. By following this approach, the level of tension will remain consistent when you resume reading.

- Make sure to carefully review each row for any errors. If you come across any, discard and begin anew.

- Knitting swatches can provide valuable insights into the appearance of the final product, particularly when working with novelty yarn.

- Before starting your project, it is a good idea to practice new techniques with scrap yarn. This will help you avoid any headaches or frustration down the line.

- Remember to keep a small ball of the yarn you used, properly labeled, for future repairs.

- For a neat finish to your crochet project, consider using a yarn needle to weave the ends back through instead of a crochet hook. This will help ensure their security and minimize the risk of unraveling.

- When selecting yarns, it is important to keep in mind that even if two yarns have the same gauge, they may not be easily interchangeable. It is particularly crucial if you wish to make any alterations to the pattern.

- It is a good idea to purchase additional yarn before beginning your project, just in case you run out and are unable to find the exact same dye lot later on.

- Choose the perfect yarn to complement or enhance the desired effect of your stitch.

- When working with a more intricate yarn, it is best to opt for a simpler project shape and pattern stitch.

- For threading fraying or stubborn yarn, try dipping the end in clear nail polish. Make sure to tightly twist the yarn as it dries.

- The drape and feel of the final product may vary based on factors such as the type of fiber used, the tightness of the spin, and the dye color.

- If you are unsure, it is always a good idea to reach out to a team member who has expertise in this area. They can help ensure that your final project closely matches the pattern image, especially if you plan on using a different type of yarn.

- Make sure to complete a row before you put your work aside. Otherwise, you might notice a change in tension the next time you pull it up.

- Utilize modeling clay to enhance the manageability of your hooks. Shape the clay within the handle, and then hold it in your preferred manner. Follow the instructions and there you have it! Personalized handles.

- Preserve your pattern by placing it in a plastic sheet protector and utilize a dry-erase marker to keep track of rows on the plastic. Utilize a binder clip to ensure the pattern remains in place, preventing any unwanted movement of the paper and protector.

- To conceal stitches, simply take the end of the stitch and crocheting it into the surrounding stitches a few times.

- When working with crochet stitches that have multiple loops, it is helpful to pull them up lightly so that it is easier to draw through them.

- To prevent any unsightly holes or loose stitches, simply start a new yarn at the start of a row. If you happen to run out of yarn while in the middle of a row, simply remove that row of staples and connect with the new yarn at the border where the connection will be less noticeable.

Chapter 3
Pro Tips and Crochet Techniques

Here, I'll give you my insider tips on how to advance your crochet knowledge and abilities so you can crochet like a master. Use my easy crochet knowledge-boosting methods to crochet more quickly and effortlessly. I also offer advice on how to select the best crochet hook for your needs and how to use your yarn more efficiently.

Expert Advice on Yarn Handling

Get valuable tips on yarn handling in crochet to enhance your skills and steer clear of common errors. Here are some helpful tips:

- Discover a cozy method for gripping your yarn: There are various methods for holding your yarn, and it is crucial to discover a technique that suits your comfort.

- Mastering tension: Dealing with tension can be quite exasperating when it comes to learning crochet. However, fret not, as there are various tips along tricks to help you gain control over your tension. Try out various techniques for holding your yarn to discover the most effective method for you.

- Prevent poor crochet techniques: Several mistakes to steer clear of are yarning under instead of over, neglecting to count stitches, and crocheting into the incorrect part of the stitch.

- Ensure you select the appropriate crochet hook size: Using an incorrect hook size may result in stitches that are either too tight or too loose.

- Properly weaving in ends: Ensuring that you weave in your ends thoroughly after completing a project is crucial to maintaining its structural integrity.

- Make sure to carefully review the pattern: It is important to thoroughly review the pattern before beginning to prevent any errors.

- Keep track of your stitches: Regularly counting your stitches will help you stay on course and ensure that you are after the pattern accurately.

- Address errors promptly: When a mistake occurs, it is crucial to rectify it promptly to avoid any further complications.

By following these valuable tips, you can enhance your yarn-caring skills and create stunning crochet projects.

Stretching Your Crochet Skills

Here are a few methods to expand your crochet abilities:

- Experiment with different stitching techniques: Explore different stitches to enhance your crochet abilities and craft intricate projects.

- Let us work on improving your skills in increasing and decreasing: Mastering the art of increasing and decreasing in crochet is crucial for shaping your work and unleashing a world of possibilities in terms of patterns and designs.

- Expand your crochet: If you complete a crochet project and discover that the stitches are too snug, you can loosen them by blocking your work. Wet-blocking is a technique used to gently relax stitches by dampening them and carefully pinning them into the desired shape.

- Mastering your tension: Tension can be a challenging aspect of learning to crochet, but fear not! There are various tips and tricks that can assist you in gaining control over your tension. Try out various techniques for holding your yarn to discover the most effective method for you.

- Join a crochet community: Being a part of a crochet community can provide you with the opportunity to expand your skill set, receive valuable feedback on your projects, and establish connections with fellow enthusiasts.

By exploring different stitching techniques, honing your ability to increase and decrease stitches, perfecting your tension control, and connecting with fellow crochet enthusiasts, you can enhance your crochet abilities and craft stunning projects.

Creative Techniques and Strategies

Here are some innovative techniques and methods of crochet:

- Focus on quantity rather than quality: Emphasize producing a larger volume of crochet projects to enhance your skills at a faster pace. This involves dedicating additional time to crocheting and creating a greater number of projects.

- Mastering the art of increasing and decreasing is crucial in crochet. These techniques allow you to manipulate your work, giving it shape and enabling you to experiment with various patterns and designs.

- Stretch your crochet: If you complete a crochet project and discover that the stitches are too tight, you can easily loosen them by blocking your work.

- Explore colorwork techniques: Experiment with a variety of colors and patterns in crochet by delving into different colorwork methods, such as tapestry crocheting and intarsia crochet.

- Join a crochet community: Being part of a crochet community can provide you with opportunities to expand your skillset, receive valuable feedback on your creations, and establish connections with fellow crocheters.

- Try out different loops: Explore the possibilities of working in various loops, like the back loop only (BLO) and front loop only (FLO) crochet, to achieve unique textures and patterns.

- Discover new stitches: Explore different stitches to enhance your crochet abilities and craft intricate projects.

- Consider utilizing different materials: Explore the possibilities of using unconventional materials like wire and fabric to craft one-of-a-kind crochet projects.

Through exploring various stitches, honing your skills in increasing and decreasing, and embracing a range of techniques and supplies, you can expand your crochet abilities and produce stunning and one-of-a-kind projects.

Chapter 4
Crocheting for All: Right and Left-Hander

There are individuals who prefer using their right hand, while others favor their left hand. Which one are you and which grasp do you crochet with? Let us explore the differences between them!

Crocheters who are left-handed and right-handed work in opposing directions:

- A crocheter who prefers using their right hand will crochet in rows coming from right to left along with in the round in an anticlockwise direction.
- A crocheter who prefers using their left-hand works a row compared to left to right and in the round clockwise.

A crochet project made by a left-handed person would be a mirror image of the same task made by a right-handed person. For instance, a basic pattern of rows of double crochet created by a crocheter who is left-handed will appear mirrored compared to the same pattern made by a right-handed crocheter. It would require careful scrutiny to detect any distinctions between the two.

Techniques for Right-Hander

Here are a few crochet techniques that may be helpful for those who crochet with their right hand:

- Wait a moment: Grasp the wide bar of the connect with your right hand, just like you would hold a pencil
- Adhere to established writing structures: It is possible to do right-handed crochet using both written structures and visual ones.
- Explore various stitches: Explore a range of stitches, including single crochet, double crochet, as well as treble crochet, to enhance your crochet abilities

- Work in rows from right to left: Crocheters typically work in rows from right to left and in the round clockwise
- Check out these helpful video tutorials: Check out video tutorials for a fresh perspective on learning novel methods and stitches

By mastering the proper technique, following instructions, honing various stitches, and utilizing online tutorials, individuals can enhance their crochet abilities and produce stunning projects.

Techniques for Left-Hander

Here are a few crochet techniques specifically for those who crochet with their left hand:

- Get ready: Get ready to start by holding the hook in your left grasp and the thread in your right hand
- Follow written structures Left-handed crochet can be done using both written designs and visual ones.
- When crocheting, it is important to work in rows from left to right. This applies to both left-handed crocheters and those working in the round anticlockwise.
- Check out video tutorials: Explore video tutorials tailored for left-handers to discover fresh techniques and stitches
- Explore various stitches: Experiment with a range of stitches, including single stitch, double stitch, and treble stitch, to enhance your crochet abilities

By mastering the proper technique, following instructions, honing various stitches, and utilizing specialized video tutorials, left-handers can enhance their crochet abilities and produce stunning projects.

3: CROCHET PATTERN IDEAS and PROJECTS VOL. 1 (BEGINNER-FRIENDLY)

Crochet projects for beginners

If you are new to crochet, similar to my experience a few months ago, you might feel a bit overwhelmed by the abundance of project ideas available. Perhaps you could use some guidance in determining where to begin. Ever since I started crocheting, I have experimented with a variety of patterns that are perfect for beginners. Today, I am excited to share some of my favorites with you! I hope you find some inspiration to begin your next project. In this section, we will discuss some basic patterns for beginners to get started with easy steps.

Chapter 1
Easy Crochet Washcloth

This crochet washcloth pattern is perfect for beginners. It is a fast project that gives you the opportunity to learn a new stitch while creating something practical!

The crochet stitch used in this pattern has a lovely, understated texture. Textured stitches can sometimes use up more yarn than other stitches. On the other hand, the single crochet bobble stitch is completely different.

To create this washcloth, you will only need to be familiar with a few fundamental crochet stitches, such as the half-double crochet and slip stitch. If you have a good grasp of these stitches and feel confident using them, you should have no problem finishing this project.

Method

- Row 1: Begin by making a slip stitch in the second chain from the hook, followed by a half-double crochet in the next chain. Perform a slip stitch in the next stitch, followed by a half-double crochet in the next stitch. Continue to alternate slip stitches and half-double crochets across the row. Make sure to complete the row by making a slip stitch in the last chain stitch. Ch 1 and move.
- Choose the size that works best for you, whether it is rows 2-35 or any other size you prefer. Begin by working a slip stitch in the first stitch, followed by a half-double crochet in the next stitch. Continue the pattern throughout the entire row. Complete a slip stitch in the final stitch. Ch 1 and move.
- Border (optional)
- When you reach your preferred size: Ch 1, turn. Insert a single crochet stitch into the first stitch and every stitch around the washcloth. Place SC, Ch 1, SC into each corner. Join the last stitch to the first stitch to complete the round. Finish off and neatly secure all loose ends.

Chapter 2
Crochet Easy Scarf

This straightforward scarf pattern is perfect for beginners. It utilizes a simple stitch and can be completed quickly.   This crocheted simple scarf is perfect for beginners in crocheting as it only requires one stitch - the single crochet!

Single crochet stitches are incredibly easy to learn and provide a wonderful opportunity for crocheters to hone their skills in this delightful craft.

Method

- Foundation Row: Ch 11 using very bulky yarn.
- Row 1: Sc first in the second ch from the hook and once in each ch across to start the next row (10)
- Row 2: SC in first st (not in ch 1), turn work, sc once in each st across to begin row 2. (10).
- Repeat row 2 (10) to complete row 3-101.
- Using a yarn needle, weave in slack yarn ends across the scarf after row 101, the final row, and use scissors to fasten off the yarn.
- Optional: To create a crocheted infinity scarf, join the scarf's two ends together.

Chapter 3
Twisted Ear Warmer Crochet

Another popular among novice crochet projects are these lovely and useful crochet ear warmers. This headband pattern for ear warmers is made with simple crochet stitches, but it looks more sophisticated thanks to the twist element added. There are multiple size variations available for this design, including medium, large, and small sizes for ladies, teens, and children. Perfect for all novices!

Method

- 12 stitches make up the chain.
- Single crochet: Work a single crochet in each chain across and in the second chain from the hook. Eleven stitches
- Turn and chain: Turn and chain one.
- Single crochet: Make a single crochet in each stitch across, but just in the back loop. Eleven stitches
- Steps 3 and 4 should be repeated until the piece is 19 inches long.
- Twist: Twist the piece once, then use a slip stitch to secure the two ends together.
- Single crochet: Work one stitch through each of the headband's two loops for each stitch.
- Finish: Weave in the ends and fasten off.

Chapter 4
Crochet Bobble Headband

Crafting a headband is a simple and straightforward project that is perfect for those who are new to crocheting. This project can be completed in no time at all and requires only a small amount of yarn.   I thoroughly enjoyed creating this pattern.   I absolutely love the knobby texture in my crochet, and this project definitely delivers on that front!   Basic crochet stitches are used throughout - only single along with double crochets are needed to create this textured masterpiece!

Method

- Create a sufficient number of stitches to encircle your head at the location where a headband would typically be worn. It should have a comfortable fit, without being overly constricting.
- Connect the ends of the chain together using a slip stitch, ensuring that your stitches remain untwisted.
- Make sure to single-crochet through each loop of each stitch onto the headband.
- Continue with step 3 till the headband reaches the desired width.
- Finish off and neatly secure the loose ends.

The simple headband is a straightforward and effortless project that is ideal for those just starting out. With just a few simple stitches, you can easily make a fashionable and warm accessory for the wintertime season.

Chapter 5
Easy Baby Blanket

Are you in search of exquisite crochet baby blanket structures that are a breeze to crochet? This baby blanket has a lovely texture and is incredibly soft and squishy. And... It is incredibly simple!

This crochet pattern provides an easy way to make cozy blankets for the precious little ones in your life. The pattern features two of the most fundamental crochet stitches: the single crochet stitch and the double crochet stitch. This at-ease beginner baby wrap crochet pattern requires only a small amount of yarn.

Method

- Using a 6mm crochet hook, start by chaining 110 stitches or any even number of chains to create the width of the baby blanket. For this example, I linked 12 together.
- Row 1: Begin by using a 5mm hook and working a slip stitch in the next chain from your hook.
- Perform a half double knit in the following chain.
- Continue across the row. Make sure to finish off with a slip stitch.
- Complete the first chain and then turn in your work.
- Row 2: Begin by working a slip stitch in the first stitch, which is the same as the slip stitch in the previous row.
- Perform a half-double crochet in the following stitch, which should be placed on top of the half-double crocheting in the previous row.
- Continue alternating slip stitches along with half double crochets throughout the row.
- Finish off with a slip stitch in the final stitch. Complete the first chain stitch and then turn your work. Continue repeating row 2 until you achieve the size you want.

Chapter 6
Crochet Tips for newbie's

Here are a few crochet tips for beginners:

- Take it easy with your stitches: Make sure to keep your stitches at ease and loose to prevent your work from becoming too tight

- Repetition is crucial: Repeating your crochet techniques is essential for enhancing your skills. With consistent practice, your skills will continue to improve

- Let us begin with the fundamentals: Begin with the basic stitches and gradually progress to more intricate projects

- Explore a variety of resources: Explore various sources, including books, websites, and video instructions, to gain a comprehensive understanding of crochet

- Join a crochet community: Working for a crochet community can provide you with opportunities to learn new skills, receive valuable feedback on your work, and connect with fellow crocheters.

- Utilize the appropriate resources: Ensure that you use the appropriate tools, such as the correct size grasp and yarn, to achieve the desired outcome for your project

- It is important to have patience when it comes to crocheting as it can be a time-consuming process. It is important to stay positive even if your work does not meet your expectations initially. Keep honing your skills and you will see progress

By following these helpful suggestions, beginners can enhance their crochet competencies and craft stunning projects.

4: CROCHET PATTERN IDEAS and PROJECTS VOL. 2 (INTERMEDIATE)

Crochet projects for Intermediate

Intermediate crocheters have developed their skills and are now prepared to take on more complex and detailed projects. Consider exploring more intricate stitches such as cables, textured patterns, or colorwork. The intermediate level opens up a world of possibilities for crochet enthusiasts, allowing them to explore their creativity and try out new techniques. It is an exciting stage that offers ample opportunities to expand your crafting skills. With perseverance and experience, crocheters at an intermediate level can create exquisite, timeless pieces that highlight their commitment and expertise.

Let's try these projects!

Chapter 1
Bavarian Crochet

Are you interested in discovering a fresh stitch combination that produces vibrant crochet squares? Discover the world of Bavarian crochet. Beginning with a cross shape at the center, the interconnected rounds of Bavarian crochet seamlessly merge, and enabling you to create beautiful gradients and make good use of any extra yarn you may have.

This intermediate method is a relatively new stitch that bears a resemblance to Catherine's Wheel, but it stands out due to its distinctive method of connecting the rounds. You might even feel a nostalgic touch as your work progresses.

Method

- Begin by chaining 4 stitches and then join them with a slip stitch to create a ring.
- Step 1: Begin by chaining 1 and then proceed to create 12 single crochet stitches into the ring. Connect with a slip stitch to the initial single crochet.
- Next step: Begin by chaining 1 and then single crocheting into the first single crochet from the previous round. Connect two chains and skip the following single crochet stitch. Insert your hook into the following single crochet stitch, create a chain of two, and skip the subsequent single crochet stitch. Continue the pattern from * to * all the way around. Connect with a slip stitch to the initial single crochet.
- Round 3: Begin by chaining 1 and then single crochet into the first chain-2 space from round two. Continue by chaining 2 and single crocheting into the next chain-2 space. Continue the pattern by chaining 2, then single crocheting into the next chain-2 space, and repeating this process. Continue the pattern from * to * around. Connect with a slip stitch to the initial single crochet.

- Round 4: Begin by chaining 1 and then single crochet into the first chain-2 space from round three. Chain 2 and single crochet into the next chain-2 space. Continue the pattern by chaining 2, single crocheting into the next chain-2 space, chaining 2, and single crocheting into the next chain-2 space. Continue the pattern from * to * around. Connect with a slip stitch to the initial single crochet.

- Round 5: Begin by chaining 1 and then single crochet into the first chain-2 space from round four. Continue by chaining 2 and single crocheting into the next chain-2 space. Continue the pattern by chaining 2, single crocheting into the next chain-2 space, chaining 2, single crocheting into the next chain-2 space, chaining 2, single crocheting into the next chain-2 space, and chaining 2, single crocheting into the next chain-2 space. Continue the pattern from * to * around. Connect with a slip stitch to the initial single crochet.

- Round 6: Begin by chaining 1 and then single crochet into the first chain-2 space from round five. Continue by chaining 2 and single crocheting into the next chain-2 space. Continue the pattern by chaining 2, single crocheting into the next chain-2 space, and repeating this sequence for the remaining chain-2 spaces. Continue the process from * to * around. Connect by using a slip stitch to the initial single crochet.

- Round 7: Begin by chaining 1 and then single crochet into the first chain-2 space from round six. Continue by chaining 2 and single crocheting into the next chain-2 space. Continue the pattern by single crocheting into each chain-2 space and chaining 2 in between. Continue the pattern from one point to another, repeating it all the way around. Connect with a slip stitch to the initial single crochet.

- Round 8: Begin by chaining 1 and then single crochet into the first chain-2 space from round seven. Continue by chaining 2 and single crocheting into the next chain-2 space. Continue the pattern by chaining 2 and single crocheting into each chain-2 space. Continue the process from * to * around. Connect by using a slip stitch to the initial single crochet.

- Round 9: Begin by chaining 1 and then single crochet into the first chain-2 space from round eight.   Continue by chaining 2 and then single crocheting into the next chain-2 space.   Continue the pattern of chaining 2 and single crocheting into each chain-2 space.   Continue the pattern from * to * all the way around.   Connect with a slip stitch to the initial single crochet.

- Round 10: Begin by chaining 1 and then single crochet into the first chain-2 space from round nine.   Continue by chaining 2 and single crocheting into the next chain-2 space.   Continue the pattern by single crocheting into each chain-2 space and chaining 2 in between.   Continue the pattern from one point to another, repeating it all the way around.   Connect with a slip stitch to the initial single crochet.

- Finish up: Finish up by fastening off and weaving in the ends.

The Bavarian stitch square is a stunning and detailed crochet pattern that can be utilized to make blankets, scarves, and various other projects.   Through consistent practice, one can become skilled in this particular stitch and produce truly remarkable projects.

Chapter 2
Crochet Snowdrift Hat

The Snowdrift Hat is a cozy beanie pattern available in four different sizes: Toddler, Child, Teen/Adult Small, and Adult Large. It is created by crocheting a rectangular and then stitching the ends and top together to achieve the beanie shape!

Here's a step-by-step guide on creating a snowdrift hat. You have the option to personalize it by incorporating various shades and stitching techniques to create a snowdrift effect. Here is a simple pattern:

Method

- First, let us start with the Crown.
- Begin by creating a magical ring or chain 4 and connect it with a slip stitch to form a ring.
- Begin by chaining 3, which will serve as your first double crochet. Proceed to work 11 additional double crochets into the ring. Make sure you have a total of 12 double crochets.
- Join the round by slipping the stitch into the top of the initial chain 3.
- Remember to place a stitch marker in the last stitch of the round to easily mark the end of each round.
- Next Step: Boost the Number of Rounds
- Begin by chaining 3, which will serve as the first double crochet.
- Additionally, you can work another double crochet in the same stitch.
- Keep going by working two double crochets in every stitch around. In this round, there will be a total of 24 double crochets.
- Join the round by slip stitching to the top of the initial chain 3.
- To begin the next round, chain 3 (this will serve as the first double crochet).
- Work another double crochet in the same stitch.
- One double crochet in the next stitch, followed by two double crochets in the next stitch. Continue the process from * to * around.
- Join the round by slip stitching to the top of the initial chain 3. There will be a

total of 36 double crochets in this round.

- Step 3: Constructing the Hat's Body
- To create the body of the hat, start by chaining 3, which will serve as the first double crochet.
- Perform 1 double crochet in every stitch around.
- Keep following this pattern for as many rounds as needed to reach the height you want for your hat.
- Step 4: Let us now move on to creating the Snowdrift Pattern.
- To achieve the snowdrift texture, you can switch between front-post double crochets (fpdc) and back-post double crochets (bpdc) for a few rounds. This gives the hat a textured appearance.
- You have the freedom to repeat the fpdc and bpdc rounds as many times as you desire in order to achieve the snowdrift effect. Usually, completing 2-4 rounds of this pattern should suffice.
- Step 5: Complete the Hat
- To complete the hat, you can add a round of single crochet stitches to the brim for a polished finish. If you would like, you can also add a pom-pom on top.
- Trim the yarn, making sure to leave a small piece. Take the yarn and carefully thread it through a yarn needle. Then, skillfully weave in the loose ends to ensure they are securely fastened.

Congratulations! Your Snowdrift Hat is now complete! This is a simple template that can be personalized with your preferred colors and enhanced with decorations or extra textures to suit your preferences. Embrace the warmth and comfort of your handmade hat!

Chapter 3
Party Bunting

Creating triangles is an excellent method for honing your skills in single crochet increases.   Start with a few stitches and gradually increase at both ends until you achieve the desired triangular shape.   Bunting is a fantastic project for making the most of the shapes that are created.

Method

- With yarn A, make 6 triangles; with yarn B and C, make 5 triangles each. Do two ch.
- ROW1: SC 1 into the second chain from the hook.
- ROW 2 Ch 1, 3 sts into the following st.
- Ch 1, sc in each sc to finish in ROW 3.
- ROW 4 Ch 1, sc to final sc, 2 sc in last sc. (5-star)
- To reach 25 stitches, repeat the final two rows.

- Work on these 25 sts straight for 6 rows; do not turn; instead, work 2 more stitches into the last sc. Work equally in sc down the point's edge; work 3 sc into the triangle's point; work evenly in sc up the other side of the point; join to the top row of sc with a ss. Bind yarn ends and weave in.

- Work a chain of 13 3/4 in (35 cm) length with yarn D. Next, work evenly in sc along the top of one triangle with yarn A. Next, work 10 ch and work in sc along a triangle with yarn B. Finally, work 10 ch and work in sc along a triangle with yarn C. Proceed in this manner, connecting the triangles using this sequence of colors, and end with a red triangle.

- Work a 14-inch (36-cm) long ch, and turn. For the first triangle, skip 10 chains, sc into the next chain, and so on.

- Work in single crochet along the triangles and chains to the last six chains, then work one single crochet into the last chain.

- Bind yarn ends and weave in.

Chapter 4
Child's Crocheted Hood

Use Germantown worsted or eiderdown with a hook big enough to hold the wool without fraying. Sew in 4 chains, and then join.

Method

- Chain 3: Draw a loop through the second and third stitches of the chain, and another through the ring; take up the wool and work off all at once; chain 1 to close the star; draw a loop through the star's eye (under the chain you just made); another through the back portion of the previous loop; work off as before; repeat until you have made six stars; join.

- Work 12 stars in the row, placing the fourth loop of each star in the last stitch of the star before it and the fifth loop in the stitch ahead, so that you have two stars above each star in the row before it.

- Create 16 stars with 4 widths.

- Work back and forth for 3 rows, leaving 4 stars for the back of the neck. To ensure that the stars appear on the correct side, break the wool at the end of each row and fasten in at the beginning. Chain 3, then pull two loops through the second and third stitches of the chain, continuing as normal.

- Create four rows of doubles around the bottom border, and then encircle the hood with a row of stars, extending to include an extra star at each front corner to keep drawing from happening.

- Chain 3, join; chain 7, * a double treble in ring; chain 3, repeat from * six times; join to the fourth chain of the seven chains. This is the rosette. Finish with ribbon ties, stitch the rosette in place, and run the ribbon in and out of the gaps.

This hood is simply increased by following basic instructions, and it may be made with any type of stitch—plain or decorative.

Chapter 5
Child's Cap in Bean-Stitch

One skein of cream-white Shetland floss and a small amount of light-blue Saxony yarn, along with a medium-sized bone hook, are needed. Chain 5; connect.

Method

- Work in a quarter-inch loop, yarn over, hook in the ring, draw loop through, over, and draw through three loops on the needle; * chain 1, work in a loop in the ring, over, draw up another loop in the ring, over, draw through all four loops; work in this manner to create four more bean stitches, or six in total, with one chain in between; join last chain to the top of the first stitch.

- To create the first stitch of each row, pull a loop up long over the first bean stitch, over, hook through the same stitch, draw through, over, and draw through all the loops. Begin with a single chain, then work a bean stitch in the area that follows.

57

Continue this pattern around, then join.

- Join every third bean stitch, in the first stitch, every space, and every chain in between.
- Bead stitch over every fourth bean stitch, same as the third row.
- Similar to the fourth row, but with a space added in between widenings; in the fifth row, create a bean stitch every fifth, and so on, in the tenth row, a bean stitch every tenth.
- Work a bean stitch into every area.
- Switch to double crochet, working a double in every stitch, for the headband.
- Working in both veins of the stitch, a double in each double; narrow twice in each row.
- Double in every other double.
- Each 2d double has a bean stitch with 1 chain in between.
- In every empty area, bean stitch; cut off white yarn.
- Attach blue yarn in space, chain 4, draw up a loop from the hook in the second chain, one in the third and one in the fourth, all fairly long loops, over, draw through all four loops, chain 1, attach single in next spot, and repeat. This finishes the edge of the cap and creates a little, pointed scallop.
- About the pushpin: Chains 3 and 8 doubles in the second chain stitch using the blue yarn. Without joining, continue around and around. Work 2 doubles in each stitch for the first row, then widen the work to almost the same size as the button you want to cover. After a round or two, decrease by working off 3 loops instead of 2, slip the button in and work tight over the button until you have covered about half of the space. Break the yarn, draw up with the needle, and sew to the center of the crown.

This cap may be readily extended, making it big enough for a three-year-old boy or girl. For added warmth, the border can be turned down over the ears.

Chapter 6
Other Simple Projects

Here are some simple and easy projects to try:

A Pretty Neck Tie

Begin by casting on one hundred and forty loops. Work one row with each color, alternating between three rows of white and five rows of colored yarn. This combination will create a sufficiently wide necktie. Finish it by adding chenille tassels at each end.

A New Sofa Pillow

Select nine shades of double Berlin wool. Begin by casting on eighty loops, and start with the darkest shade. Crochet one row with each color, progressing from the darkest to the lightest, and then back to the darkest. You can create a shaded effect by including white rows in between. Aim for about three complete stripes, making the pillow approximately half a yard square. You can choose to crochet both sides of the pillow or use silk for the back.

A Carpet Bag

Start by casting on sixty loops and work in plain double crochet using double Berlin wool. For the border on each side, consider a narrow border with green leaves, about ten to twelve stitches wide, set on a scarlet background. In the center, use black ground and create a diamond arabesque pattern using bright gold, scarlet, green, and blue.

The bag should be about half a yard wide overall, with the border on the other side. You can vary the pattern for the rest of the bag as you prefer. Complete the bag with patent leather sides and a bottom, along with a steel frame at the top. When working with patterns, make sure to pass the whole pattern between the needle and the yarn you're working with.

Neck Rest or Cushion

These are particularly comfortable for invalids and are typically made using shaded wool in six colors, such as scarlet, green, lilac, orange, blue, and drab. Cast on ninety loops and work eight rows in each color. Use plain double crochet. When you cast on the loops for the foundation, join the ends and work in the round. Finish the neck rest or cushion with velvet ends and two pieces of cord around each piece of velvet. Black cord often looks better than colored.

A Brioche or Turkish Cushion:

Start by casting on thirty loops with black wool and crochet four rows all around, increasing one stitch at the end of each row. Then, use a skein of shaded double Berlin wool. Start one stitch below the point of the black and work around to the top of the other side. Begin four loops below and work until you are within four loops of the other side.

Repeat this process for eight rows, decreasing three loops each time. You'll need to make twelve pieces in this manner, and using different colors for each piece makes it even prettier. Repeat the colors once you've finished the first set. Crochet them all together for six rows around the bottom, and make a round cushion to cover. Finish it with a Brioche mount in the center.

A Very Elegant Bag

To create this elegant bag, begin by casting on three hundred loops. Crochet six plain rows in black. Then, thread your beads onto the blue silk yarn and crochet a section. When adding the beads, pass your needle through the loop, slide a bead close to the stitch, and complete it. After finishing the beaded section, crochet twelve plain rows in blue and six in black. The seventh and eighth rows should be done in plain open crochet.

To allow the cord to pass through, select a pattern that is about forty to fifty rows deep. You can also create round bags by starting with three stitches and increasing every other stitch for the first six rounds, followed by increasing every third stitch for the next twelve rounds, and so on until the bottom is the desired size. Continue adding rounds to achieve the desired bag size. Stripes of different colors, combined with beads or patterns in contrasting colors on every other stripe, make for a lovely design.

Chapter 7
Crochet Tips for Intermediate

For crocheters who are intermediate, try these tips:

- Put yourself to the test: Experiment with different stitches, patterns, and methods to push your abilities and gain new knowledge.

- Study from many sources: Learn from a variety of resources to obtain a comprehensive understanding of crochet, including books, blogs, and video lessons.

- Join a crochet group: Making new friends, learning new techniques, and receiving criticism on your work are all made possible by participating in a crochet community.

- Try experimenting with different yarns: Examine how various yarn kinds impact the appearance and feel of your creations.

- Take on more ambitious tasks: Take on more difficult projects to push yourself and develop your abilities, like blankets or sweaters.

- Practice tension control: To guarantee smooth and consistent stitches, practice managing your tension.

- Employ stitch markers: To ensure accuracy and maintain track of your stitches, use stitch markers.

- Shut down your projects. Your completed projects will appear more polished and professional if you block them.

Intermediate crocheters are able to continue to develop their abilities and produce stunning projects by setting challenges for themselves, learning from various sources, becoming a member of a crochet community, testing with yarns, taking on larger projects, honing tension control techniques, using stitch markers, and blocking their work.

5: CROCHET PATTERN IDEAS and PROJECTS VOL. 3 (ADVANCED)

Chapter 1
Ladies' Sweater

Method

Five skeins of knitting-worsted and four balls of Angora are needed for this sweater; the model used gray Angora and electric blue for the body of the garment, but you can use any other color you like. The work is done in back-and-forth plain knitting with a ribbed belt. Cast on 119 stitches for the back (it will measure around twenty-four inches) using the knitting-worsted and No. 5 needles. Knit 48 ribs or 96 rows.

* Narrow, knit 4 in the next row; repeat from *. Next, switch to No. 12 steel needles and work 20 rows for the belt in triple rib (knit 3, purl 3). Knit 20 ribs using No. 5 needles; drop 1 stitch at the needle end every other row for five rows. Work 29 ribs in a plain or non-decreasing pattern.

Cast on 30 stitches at the neck, knit 29 ribs, increase 1 stitch at the armhole every other row five times, and crochet 22 ribs plain. The following row consists of 34 stitches, 34 stitches are knitted, a spare needle is slipped into the working needle, and 21 stitches are bound off for the neck. The working needle is then transferred to the spare needle. Make the switch to the steel needles, and beginning at the front edge of the belt, stitch the belt according to the instructions for the back (purl 3, knit 3).

After you have completed the belt, which consists of twenty rows of triple ribs, move to needle size No. 5, knit four stitches, increase by one stitch, and then repeat the pattern from *. After that, knit 48 ribs, but make sure to bind off on the wrong side. If you are going to use buttonholes, you should knit the matching front before you make the buttonholes.

Work an additional stitch into each rib all the way around the armhole on the right side of the sweater, bringing the total number of stitches for the sleeve up to 72. Knit eight rows of ribbing, then decrease one stitch at each end of the needle after every eighth row of ribbing for a total of eight times. Knit 12 ribs with steel needles for the wrist, then move to larger needles (No. 5) and knit 4 narrow stitches. Repeat these steps across the row. Knit 12 ribs, then knit 7 ribs after joining the Angora and bind off.

Cast on 65 stitches with the knitting worsted and knit twenty-eight ribs with needles size No. 5. This will create the collar. After joining the Angora wool, knit 11 rows while increasing the stitch count by 1 at both ends of the needle every other row, and then tie off. While focusing on the right side of the collar, pick up one stitch on each side rib, knit 11 rows while increasing one stitch every other row toward the corner and keeping an even neck edge, and then bind off. Finish off the mitered corners with several stitches, and then match up the other side of the collar. By working additional rows or ribs into the pattern, angora wool borders can be expanded to any width that the wearer requires.

The belt is secured in place by two substantial buttons, each of which is encased in either knitted or crocheted yarn and features a loop that is sewn on both sides. Concerning the button: Make a chain of three stitches with the bone hook that will hold the yarn, turn, and make eight doubles in the subsequent stitch of the chain; in the next round, make a pair of doubles in each stitch, working in both directions to prevent ribs; then make one double in the initial stitch, two doubles in the next stitch, and so on. This pattern will create a ribbed pattern.

Work in a continuous round without increasing, slide in the mold, then skip 1 stitch and make a double crochet in the next, repeating this pattern until the cover is closed. Continue working around until you form a circle large enough to cover the button mold—five rounds were required for the top of the buttons used on the model. Optionally, knit a small square of the same size as the garment's body. Use this square to cover the mold, pulling it snugly over and sewing it in place from below. To create a loop, make a chain of thirty stitches, turn, and double each stitch; securely attach it under the button.

Chapter 2
Collar—Bouquet

Using Taylor's Crochet Thread, No. 12, and Needle No. 23 with a Bell Gauge, all stitches not worked in the chain should be Double Crochet.

Method

Method For the FIRST SMALL LEAF:

- Create a chain of 10 stitches, then turn.
- Skip 4 stitches, and in the 5th stitch, work a single stitch to create a rounded loop. Then, turn back.
- Leave the initial chain for the stem and continue by working 7 chains in the round loop, followed by 1 plain stitch, 9 chains, 1 plain stitch, and 7 chains. Then, turn back.
- Skip 1 stitch and work (4 chains and 1 plain stitch, repeated 7 times) in the 7-chain loop. Then, skip 1 stitch and work 1 plain stitch in the 9-chain loop.
- Continue by working (4 chains and 1 plain stitch, repeated 7 times) in the 9-chain loop, then skip 1 stitch and work 1 plain stitch in the 7-chain loop.
- Finish the leaf by working (4 chains and 1 plain stitch, repeated 7 times) in the 7-chain loop.
- Work 5 single stitches down the stem.

For the SECOND SMALL LEAF:

- Create a chain of 10 stitches, then turn.
- Skip 4 stitches, and in the 5th stitch, work a single stitch to create a rounded loop. Then, turn back.
- Leave the initial chain for the stem and continue by working 7 chains in the round loop, followed by 1 plain stitch, 9 chains, 1 plain stitch, and 7 chains. Then, turn back.

- Work (4 chains and 1 plain stitch, repeated 3 times) in the 7-chain loop, then create 2 chains and join them to the center stitch of the 18th 4-chain loop of the 1st leaf.
- In the same 7-chain loop, work 1 plain stitch, then work (4 chains and 1 plain stitch, repeated 3 times) in the same 7-chain loop. Skip 1 stitch and work 1 plain stitch in the 9-chain loop.
- Continue by working (4 chains and 1 plain stitch, repeated 7 times) in the 9-chain loop, then skip 1 stitch and work 1 plain stitch in the 7-chain loop.
- Finish the leaf by working (4 chains and 1 plain stitch, repeated 7 times) in the 7-chain loop.
- Work 5 single stitches down the stem.
- And so on for the subsequent steps.

SECTION OF COLLAR For the THIRD SMALL LEAF:

- Begin with a chain of 13 stitches and work as you did for the second small leaf. Join it to the first division of the large leaf.
- When finished, work 4 single stitches down the stem.

For the FOURTH SMALL LEAF:

- Start with a chain of 15 stitches and work as you did for the second small leaf. Join it to the center of the 18th 4-chain loop of the third leaf.
- When finished, work 6 single stitches down the stem.

For the FIFTH SMALL LEAF:

- Create a chain of 9 stitches and work as you did for the second small leaf. Join it to the center of the 18th 4-chain loop of the fourth small leaf.
- When finished, work 4 single stitches down the stem and 8 single stitches down the center stem.
- On the flower, skip 1 stitch, then work (1 plain, 6 treble, and 1 plain in the 4-chain loop), skip 1 stitch, and repeat the pattern until complete.

To start the SECOND FLOWER and CALYX:

- Begin with a chain of 14 stitches, and work as follows, just as you did for the first flower and calyx.

For the SECOND LARGE LEAF:

- Create a chain of 22 stitches and work as you did for the first large leaf, joining it to the center of the last 6 treble stitches of the first flower.
- When the leaf is finished, work 2 plain stitches down the stem and 7 plain stitches down the center stem. Then turn back.
- Create 3 chains and 1 plain stitch in each of the 5 divisions of the leaf, followed by 3 chains and 1 plain stitch at the point.
- This completes the First Pattern. When repeating it, make adjustments so that the first part of the pattern aligns with what has already been worked, keeping the shape and position of the leaves and flowers the same.

SECOND PATTERN For the first small leaf:

- Start with a chain of 10. Turn and skip 4 stitches. Work 1 single crochet, then turn back and work 7 chains.
- Followed by 1 plain stitch, 9 chains, 1 plain stitch, 7 chains, and 1 plain stitch. Turn back again.
- Next, make 4 chains and 1 plain stitch in the 7 chains twice, then 2 chains.
- Join this to the second division of the second large leaf with 2 chains and 1 plain stitch.
- Then, make 4 chains and 1 plain stitch 4 times, all in the same 7 chains.
- Skip 1 stitch and make 1 plain stitch in the 9 chains. Repeat the pattern of 4 chains and 1 plain stitch twice in the 9 chains, followed by 2 chains.
- Join this to the center of the 7th group of 6 treble stitches in the first flower.
- Make 2 chains and 1 plain stitch, then repeat the pattern of 4 chains and 1 plain stitch 4 times in the same 9 chains.
- Skip 1 stitch and make 1 plain stitch in the 7 chains.
- Repeat the pattern of 4 chains and 1 plain stitch 7 times in the 7 chains.

Finally, execute five single crochets down the stem. Proceed to craft the second small leaf and center stem as outlined in the initial pattern. Moving on to the first large leaf, create a chain of 29 stitches, turn, and skip 2 stitches. Then, work three plain stitches, followed by (2 chains, skip 2, and 1 treble 4 times), 2 chains, skip 2, and 1 plain. Turn your work, resulting in the chain stitches forming the stem. Work 1 chain to cross it. On the other side of the base, establish a 7-chain, skip 1, work 1 plain in the 2-chain foundation, skip 1, and work 1 plain in the next 2-chain. Turn back, omitting the 2 plain stitches, and execute 5 treble stitches and 1 plain in the 7-chain. Turn back once more. Proceed with a 9-chain, work 1 plain in the same 2-chain of the base as before, skip 1, work 1 plain in the next 2-chain, turn back, and skipping the 2 plain stitches, execute 7 treble stitches and 1 plain in the 9-chain.

Turn back and join it to the center of the 12th 4-chain of the first small leaf. Then, create a 7-chain, work 1 plain in the 2-chain as before, skip 1, work 1 plain, and turn back. Execute 5 treble stitches and 1 plain in the 7-chain, turn back, and join it to the 6th 6-treble of the first flower. Subsequently, form a 5-chain, work 1 plain in the 2-chain, skip 1, and work 1 plain, turning backward. Perform 3 treble stitches and 1 plain in the 5-chain, turn back, create 1 chain, skip 1, and execute 3 treble stitches on the 3 plain stitches. In the 2-chain at the point of the leaf, work 1 plain, 1 chain, connect it to the last 5 trebles of the second flower, 1 chain, and 1 plain. Turn and replicate the other side to correspond, mirroring the identical steps as in the first large leaf of the initial pattern. Conclude by executing 6 plain stitches down the stem, repeating the calyx and first flower up to the third small leaf, adhering to the same steps as in the first pattern.

For the third small leaf:

- Start with 13 chains and turn.
- Skip 4 stitches and makes 1 single crochet in the 5th stitch.
- Then, turn back and continue working in the round loop.
- Start with a series of chains and single crochets, then repeat a specific pattern multiple times.
- Connect certain chains to specific parts of the previous pattern.
- Continue with more chains and single crochets, and repeat the pattern again.
- Finish by crocheting down the stem.

- Repeat the pattern for the remaining leaves, flower, and calyx, just like in the first pattern.
- Repeat this pattern 10 more times, for a total of 12 patterns. However, when working the last pattern to create the corner, skip the 2nd flower.
- Complete the pattern, then work on the 2 small leaves and the 1 large leaf. Connect the point to the 5th small leaf.
- After that, work 20 plain stitches down the center stem.

FOR THE BAND.

For the first row, start by working 3 chain stitches and then 1 treble stitch in each of the chains along the sides of the first small and large leaves.

For the second row, start by chaining 3. Then, skip the next 3 stitches and make 1 treble crochet in the third chain from the previous row.

Repeat this pattern and finish off.

Chapter 3
Collar—Rose

Method

FOR THE ROSE

Begin by making a chain of 6 stitches, and then finish the round by functioning a single stitch in the earliest chain stitch.

For the first round, start by making a chain of 3 sutures and then continue with 1 plain stitch in the round. Repeat this process 7 times.

2d.—(Skip 3 sutures, then work 1 stitches in the 3rd stitch of the before round, repeat this 7 times).

3d.—Work 1 plain stitch, followed by 5 chain stitches, and another plain stitch. Make sure to work these plain stitches in the 3 chains of the last round. Repeat this process 6 more times.

For the 4th round, you'll want to do 2 regular stitches, followed by 1 treble stitch, and then finish off with 1 more regular stitch.   These 7 sutures should all be collaborated in the 5 chains of the previous round.

In the fifth row, you will need to make 5 single stitches, then 3 chain stitches in succession. This will complete the row. You will finish with three more single stitches after skipping the next four stitches.   Continue to repeat this pattern an additional three times, and then go back to working on the sixth row.   In order to complete the sixth row, you will need to skip one stitch, then make a plain stitch, then skip another stitch, and lastly make seven treble stitches in the three link stitches from the previous row. Perform the pattern four times, skipping one stitch between each iteration, and ending with three single stitches.

Proceed to pick up where you left off on the seventh row of work. In order to complete the seventh row, you will need to make five chain stitches, skip five stitches, and then knit three single stitches on top of the seven treble stitches from the row before it. This pattern should be repeated five times, after which you should create seven chain stitches, skip seven stitches, and then construct one plain stitch in between the two trebles from the previous round. Finally, you should produce one plain stitch, seven chain stitches, and one plain stitch.

For the 8th row, begin with a single treble stitch, then continue with 9 long stitches, and finish off with another treble stitch. All 11 stitches need to be worked in the 5 chain. Next, skip one stitch and crochet one plain stitch in the middle stitch of the three single stitches. Could you please repeat this structure 4 more times? After that, you'll want to do 8 treble stitches as well as 1 plain stitch in the seven chains. Start by skipping one plain stitch, then proceed to work one plain stitch and eight treble stitches in the seventh chain. Complete the final stitch and secure it firmly. Please complete eight of these tasks.

FOR THE LEAVES AND STEMS

Make a chain of 80 stitches for the long stem.

First, you'll want to follow the instructions carefully to develop the leaf shape by working a series of stitches. Then, on the other opposite of the foundation, keep working the pattern to finish the leaf. Be sure to carefully follow the steps to get the outcome you want. Keep going with the structure as outlined: Start by making a chain of 9 stitches, and then proceed to work a plain stitch in the next 2 chain stitches. Skip the 2 plain stitches and continue by working 7 treble stitches and 1 obvious stitch in the nine link stitches. Go back and connect it to the 29th chain stitch of the long stem. To make the leaf, start by chaining 7 stitches and then work a plain stitch in the afterward 2 chain stitches.

Return to the beginning and use the seven chain stitches to produce five treble sutures and one plain stitch. You should begin by constructing a chain consisting of 5 stitches, and after that, you should merely work a clear stitch in each of the following two chain stitches. Return to the chain threads and work three treble stitches and one plain stitch into each of those five chains. Create a chain of two stitches, then skip one stitch before beginning the next chain.

After that, crochet three treble stitches onto each of the three plain threads as well as the two chain stitches that are located at the point of the leaf. After completing one simple stitch and one chain stitch, attach the new stitch to the seventeenth chain stitches of the long stem. On the leaf, begin by working a chain stitch, and then work a plain stitch directly after the chain stitch. Adjust the other side so that it matches, as follows:

I can appreciate the time and effort you put into this hobby because I'm a crochet enthusiast myself. It's a great opportunity to show off your creative side while also producing some stunning works of art. There is always something new to learn and discover in the world of crochet, regardless of whether you are just starting out or have years of experience under your belt.

First, make 3 treble stitches, then move on to make 5 chain stitches, and finally, make 1 plain stitch in the second chain. You should now turn your work once you have skipped one stitch, created one plain stitch, and turned it. Work either three treble stitches or one plain stitch into the five-chain stitching while skipping the two stitches that are immediately following it. Repeat the process of rotating your work. Start by making seven chain stitches, then go on to one plain stitch. You can turn your work after you skip one stitch, make another plain stitch, or both.

Create 5 treble stitches and 1 plain stitch in the 7 chain stitches. Give your work one final turn. Create 9 chain stitches, followed by 1 plain stitch. Skip 1 stitch, make another plain stitch, and then turn your work. Create 7 treble sutures and 1 obvious stitch in the 9 link stitches. Rotate your work once more. Create a chain of 7 stitches, followed by a single plain stitch. Skip one stitch, then make another plain stitch. Finally, turn in your work. Create 5 treble stitches and 1 plain stitches in the 7 chain stitches.

Give your work one final turn. Finally, create 5 chain sutures and 1 plain stitch to finish the Leaf. All 5 leaves are made using the same technique, with the only difference being in how they are joined together. Make 5 single stitches lower the stem: and for the

SECOND LEAF:

Start with a 38-chain and follow the same instructions as the first leaf.

Instead of joining it to the 29th chain of the long stem, join it to the 2nd division or open space of the first leaf, always counting from the point of the leaf.

When joining at the point of the leaf, connect it to the 1st stitch of the long stem.

THIRD LEAF—34 chain:

Turn, miss 2, 3 plain, (2 chains, miss 2, and 1 treble 4 times), 2 chains, miss 2, 1 plain, turn.

Resulting in the chain stitches for the stem, work 1 chain to cross it.

On the other side of the foundation, 7 chains, miss 1, 1 plain in the 2 chains of foundation, miss 1, 1 plain in the following 2 chain, turn back, and lacking the 2 plain, work 5 treble and 1 plain in the 7 chain, turn back.

Join it to the 2d division of the 2d leaf; then 9 chains, 1 plain in the same 2 chains of the base as before, miss 1, 1 plain in the next 2 chains, turn back, and missing the 2 plain, operate 7 treble and 1 plain in the 9 chains; turn back, then 7 chains, 1 plain in the 2 chains as prior to, miss 1, 1 plain, turn back; 5 treble and 1 plain in the 7 chains, turn back; 5 chains, 1 plain in the 2 chains, miss 1, 1 plain, turn back; 3 treble, and 1 plain in the 5 chain, turn back; 1 chain, neglect 1, 3 treble on the 3 plain, and in the 2 chain at the point of the leaf, (work 1 plain, 2 chains, and 1 plain), turn, and work the other side to correspond, the same as in 1st leaf; when finished, work 8 single stitches down the stem.

FOURTH LEAF—25 chain:

Follow the same pattern as the 3d leaf, connecting it to the 4th division of the 3d Leaf.

Once completed, make 5 single stitches down the stem and 13 plain stitches down the center stem.

FIFTH LEAF—25 chain:

Turn, miss 2, 3 plain, (2 chains, miss 2 and 1 treble 4 times), 2 chains, miss 2, 1 plain, move.

Leaving the chain stitches for the stem, work 1 chain to cross it.

On the other side of the base, 7 chains, miss 1, 1 plain in the 2 chains of foundation, miss 1, 1 plain in the next 2 chains, turn back, and lacking the 2 plain, work 5 treble and 1 plain in the 7 chains, turn back.

9 chains, 1 plain in the same 2 chains of the foundation as before, miss 1, 1 plain in the next 2 chains, turn back, and missing the 2 plain, operate 7 treble and 1 plain in the 9 chain, turn back.

Then 7 chains, 1 plain in the 2 chains as before, miss 1, 1 plain, turn back; 5 treble and 1 plain in the 7 chains, turn back; 5 chains, 1 plain in the 2 chains, miss 1, 1 plain, turn back; 3 treble, and 1 plain in the 5 chains, turn back; join it to the 4th split of the 4th Leaf; 2 chains, miss 1, 3 treble on the 3 plain, and in the 2 chains at the point of the leaf, (work 1 plain, 2 chains, and 1 plain), turn, and work the other side to correspond. This completes one pattern of the Collar and should be repeated, with a slight variation: — Collar Section.

SECOND PATTERN

Make a chain of 80 links to use as the base for the long stem. Repeat steps one through three for the first, second, and third leaves of the initial design. After you have joined the third leaf to the second leaf, you will also need to link the third leaf to the second bud where there are 8 simple stitches. After that, you will need to attach the point of this plant to the stem of the smaller leaf.

The fifth leaf will be worked on next, and its point will be joined to the top of the calyx on the first bud. Continue working the fifth leaf, the rosebud, and the bud in the exact same manner as described in the First Pattern. Proceed in this manner for a total of eight patterns. Nevertheless, when you get to the last pattern, you need to build corners that are the same as the other side. After you have worked 13 single stitches down the center of the first bud, construct 40 chains and then craft a leaf that is similar to the previous leaf, only connecting it to the calyx of the bud this time. Following the designs of the third, fourth, and fifth leaves, proceeded to build three more leaves. After you have completed the project, work eight plain stitches down the central stem.

To finish the eighth design, work three single stitches along the stem of the little leaf, and then work six plain stitches down the stem of the center leaf. Proceed to the next bud, attaching the 9-chain to the base of the fourth leaf, and then move on. Work Twelve single stitches along the side of the fourth leaf after you have completed the previous step of working 15 single stitches along the side of the bud. After that, you should face the other direction and continue working the band along the remaining chains of the long stem as well as the sides of the buds.

First row: work 3 chains, skip 3 stitches, then work 1 treble; continue this pattern until the row is complete. 2d: make 3 chains, skip 3 spaces, and then work 1 treble into the chains from the row below; repeat.

3d. — Skip 2, skip 2 plain stitches in a chain of 3, continue, then tie off.

Chapter 4
Chemisette

According to the Bell Gauge, use Taylor's Crochet Yarn No. 12 and Needle No. 22 for a finer finish, or use Taylor's Crochet String No. 8 and Needle No. 20 for a coarser look. For the Point, start by making a chain of Fourteen stitches.

Method

Create a Foundation Chain First: To begin, create a foundation chain the same width as the chemisette you want. For a regular chemisette width, you might begin with a chain of 120 stitches.

Work a row of single crocheted stitches into the foundation chain to create the base row. The foundation of the lace pattern will be this row.

Choose a Lace Stitch Pattern: For your chemisette, decide on a lace stitch pattern. The chains doubled crochets, and picots can all be found in a straightforward lace pattern. This is a simple lace design to get you going:

Repeat this pattern all the way across the row: chain 3 (counts as the first double crochet), skip Two stitches, double crochet in the next stitch, loop 2, skip 2 stitches, dual crochet in the next stitch.

To make the pattern fit the design you want, adjust it.

Repeat Rows: Continue working in the lace design row until the length of your chemisette is the desired result. Whether you desire a longer undergarment or a short chemisette, you may adjust the length.

Edging: Add a decorative edge to complete your chemisette. By working a row of scallops down the bottom edge, you may create a basic scallop edge. For instance:

Repeat across the row: single crochet in the first stitch, skip two, five double crochets in the next stitch, skip two, single crochet in the next stitch.

Straps: If you would want to add buckles, you can either knit them onto the chemisette right away or add thin fabric or ribbon straps afterward.

Finishing: Shape your chemisette by blocking it and tying off any loose ends. Blocking provides the garment with a more polished appearance and aids in the lace pattern opening up.

Never forget that you may always alter the pattern to suit your tastes. Try your hand at creating a chemisette that matches your style by experimenting with various stitches and lace patterns.

Chapter 5
Crocheted Jacket

Method

This stylish jacket may be made in one or two colors, which makes it a great option for forthcoming summertime events. It provides comfort and style on chilly days and nights. Six skeins of fourfold Poplar or four skeins of one color will work for the body; if you choose a two-color design, you'll also need two yarns of white for the border.

Make a chain of 54 stitches to start, then turn. To make a total of 26 double crochets, skip 3 stitches, make 1 double crochet in the subsequent stitch, chain 1, skip 1 stitch, and repeat this pattern across the row. Flip your project. Chain 2, then double under 1 chain, chain 1, and continue the pattern all the way across. Work through the second row till you have a 22-inch-long strip that forms the back and goes all the way to the shoulder.

For one shoulder, alternate between the back and the front, repeating each row until you have nine double stitches. After four rows, turn the project around, chain two, and repeat. Expand by working 2 doubles with 1 chain in the middle of the next row. Continue this pattern in the middle of every 8th row till you have 15 doubles in total. Maintain this width until the front and back are equal in length; then, work on the nine extra doubles for the other front and reserve Eight doubles for the backside of the neck.

If you are using two colors for the border, begin with the border color at the left front corner. Under the first chain (or chain 3 for the first treble), make a treble stitch, chain 1, and then make an additional treble stitch under the next chain. To shape the collar, continue this pattern around, adding two trebles with one chain in between in the corners and across the shoulders at the neck. Using the same technique, make another row, and then continue to seed-stitch for eight rows, expanding the stitches at the corners.

Align the front and back of the garment by folding it at the shoulders. Double stitch under each chain, working your way up to 25 stitches, starting from the 10th chain from the bottom of both sides. Work around the armscye, starting from underarm, until the sleeves reach the required measurement of 12 inches. Then, use treble crochet to construct two rows of gaps as previously. Lastly, finish the sleeve by working a total of seven rows of seeds stitched to match the body of the jacket's pattern.

To create the picot edge, you will need to work two double stitches in two stitches, and then chain 3 to form a picot. Repeat this process as needed.

The stitch provided is straightforward and attractive, but feel free to choose any other decorative stitch that you prefer.   One example is the Lancaster-stitch, which is created in the following manner: With a chain of an even number of stitches, turn.

Begin by skipping the first stitch, then work a double crochet in each of the remaining stitches. Finally, turn in your work.

Start by creating a chain of 3 stitches. Next, simply yarn over and pull a loop through the initial stitch. Wrap the yarn around and pull it via the next stitch. Continue this sequence of looping the yarn over and pulling it through the stitch, then repeating the process with the next stitch. At last, complete the process by pulling the yarn through all the chains on the needle.

Start by chaining 4, and then proceed to work double knitting in the first stitches of the chain. This step will bring together or connect the group of loops. After that, you can easily create a loop by using the previous loop from the cluster. Next, simply draw a loop via the next stitch, and then draw another loop via the same stitch. Keep going by pulling a loop via the next stitch. At last, pull the yarn via all the chains on the needle. Keep doing this.

Let us discuss your project.

Begin with a double crochet in the first space, then double crochet around the thread between 4 chains and cluster. Repeat this pattern, finishing with a double crochet at the top of the 3 chains that started the last row. Reiterate the second and third rows to complete the pattern.

The bird's-eye-stitch is straightforward and enjoyable: After creating a chain of the desired length, turn.

Start by making a double stitch in each chain stitch and then turn.

Start by working a double crochet in the front loop of the stitch from the last row. Then, work another double crochet in the next stitch, this time taking the back loop. Repeat this pattern until you reach the end, and then repeat the second row.

Here's another lovely stitch that can be easily adapted to any garment: Create a series of stitches that can be divided evenly by 3, then turn.

Complete one double crochet in each remaining stitch of the chain, then turn.

Continue the pattern by adding two double crochet stitches in each double crochet stitch from the previous row. Then, turn in your work.

Start by chaining 1, then make a double crochet stitch in each of the next 2 stitches. After that, yarn over and insert the hook into the third stitch of the first row. Pull up a loop and yarn over again, then draw the yarn through the first 2 loops on the hook. Repeat this process twice more. Skip the next stitch and make a double crochet stitch in each of the next 2 stitches. Repeat these steps until you reach the end of the row, then turn your work.

Just like the second row.

Begin by chaining 1, then work a double crochet stitch in each of the first 2 double crochet stitches. Next, yarn over and make a treble crochet stitch as you did before, inserting the hook under the treble crochet stitch of the 3rd row. Skip 1 stitch, and work a double crochet stitch in each of the next 2 stitches. Repeat this pattern until you reach the end of the row, then turn in your work. Please repeat the 4th and 5th rows.

And yet another one: Create a chain of the necessary length and then rotate it. After skipping 3 stitches, you can go ahead and make 2 trebles in the afterward stitch. Keep following this pattern: skip one stitch, then create two trebles in the next stitch. Keep going through these moves until you come to the end of the row together, then turn.

Continue the pattern by chaining 3 and working 2 trebles between each group of 2 trebles in the previous row. Repeat this step. Can you please repeat the second row?

6: CROCHET PATTERN IDEAS And PROJECTS VOL. 4 (GIFTS FOR YOUR KIDS)

Chapter 1
Coat Sweater for Kids

Procedure

Materials:

- Wool
- an appropriate hook size for the wool

Front and Back Panels:

- Start by making a chain of a total of 160 stitches then turn.

- Complete one double crocheting in every stitch of the chain. Just chain 1 and give it a turn.

- Work double crochets in each double crochet, functioning in the back loop of the stitch to create a ribbed effect.

- Incorporate star stitches into the rib: Begin by chaining 3, then pull a loop through the 2nd along with 3rd stitches of the chain. Next, pull a loop through each of the 2 doubles. Take up the wool and draw it through the 5 stitches on the needle. Chain 1 to close the star. Now, draw a loop via the eye of the star (those less than the 1 chain), another by means of the back part of the endure perpendicular looping process of the same star, and finally, a loop via each of the 2 doubles. Finish the star by completing all the loops, chaining 1, and repeating until you reach the end of the row. Rotate.

- Switch back and forth between rib rows as well as rows of star-stitches, performing on the right side. The first row typically begins on the right aspect. When beginning the second row, cut the yarn at the end of the subsequent rib, secure it in place at the opposite end, create a chain of 3, and continue with the row.

- Keep following this pattern until you've completed four rows of stars as well as five rib rows. For the next row, go ahead and crochet 39 stitches, followed by a rib row. Keep doing this until you've got three rows of thirty-nine-star stitches each.

- Complete the row with double crochets, cut the yarn, and secure it firmly.

Assembly:

- Join the front and back panels in the center of the back with a single crochet, ensuring that the joining is not visible.

- Join under the arms, leaving openings for the armholes.

Border:

- Work ten rows of double crochet around the entire garment, including the fronts, bottom, and neck. Increase at each of the lower corners in each row to create a miter.

Sleeves:

- Chain 80 stitches with one additional turning chain.
- Work a rib of double crochets on the chain, followed by 40 star stitches.
- Repeat this pattern until you have ten rows of star stitches and eleven rib rows. Ensure that star stitches are always worked on the right side.
- Join the sleeve seam on the wrong side with a single crochet, as done for the back.

Buttonholes and Cuffs

- Create buttonholes in the fifth row of the front. Chain 5, skip 5 stitches, and repeat as many times as needed, ensuring the openings are evenly spaced. In the next row when working back, make a double crochet in each stitch of the 5-chain buttonhole.
- Complete 12 phases of double crocheting, making sure to work one double crocheting in each stitch and then turn back.

Final Steps:

- Sew the sleeves into the armholes.
- Attach buttons to correspond with the buttonholes on the front.
- The sweater can be resized by starting with a longer chain and making additional rows of star-stitch and rib to maintain proportion. This combination of stitches creates an attractive design.

Follow these steps carefully to create your Germantown wool sweater.

Chapter 2
Babies' Jacket

Procedure

Gathering three skeins of Saxony thread, one spindle each of silk-finished crochet-cotton and crochet-silk, and two and a half meters of No. 1 ribbon will get you started.   Choose an attachment that will gently steer the yarn in the desired direction.

Create a chain consisting of one hundred staples as a first step, and then turn it over.

To begin, you will need to skip the first four stitches. After that, you will need to work a treble stitch into each of the remaining 96 stitches. Before you do so, make sure to bring the yarn up to a height of roughly one-eighth of an inch.   To ensure that the yarn is properly finished and the item is finished appropriately, be careful to secure it and knot it off.   You may also try working with yarn instead, however, the end product might not be as amazing as working with thread would be.

Begin by fastening the thread at the point where you first started it. Pull it up, then make two trebles on top of the third treble, and finally make one treble all the way back to where you tied it in. Because of this, a cross will be formed. Continue doing so in order to end up with a total of 32 crosses. When you have finished, cut the thread in half and then rejoin it at the point where you began working on it.

Carry out 21 trebles across 7 crosses, after which carry out 12 trebles across the following 2 crossings, and finally carry out 18 trebles across 6 crosses. This pattern should be repeated twice. After that, you will need to perform 12 trebles over 2 crosses, followed by 21 trebles over 7 crosses, in order to finish the row. It is necessary to broaden the 12 trebles that are over 2, while the remaining trebles are made by placing 2 on each cross and 1 between them.

The number of crosses is the same as in the second row, which is 38.

Create 21 trebles in a plain format, with 3 trebles placed above each cross. There are 24 stitches that cross over 4, then there are 21 simple stitches. The next step consists of 21 straight stitches, which are followed by 12 crosses over 2. In the final step, 24 crosses are worked over the following 4 stitches, and then 21 plain stitches are worked after that.

There are forty-eight crosses.

Follow the given pattern step by step: make 21 stitches in a simple manner, then continue with 12 stitches that cover the next 2 crosses, and finish with another set of 12 plain stitches. After that, you'll want to repeat the sequence of 12 stitches over the next 2 crosses and 24 plain stitches twice. Keep going with 12 stitches across the next 2 crosses, followed by 12 plain stitches, and then another set of 12 stitches across the next 2 crosses. Finish the pattern by crocheting 21 stitches in a simple manner.

There are a total of fifty-eight crosses.

Perform 24 plain stitches, skip 12 crosses, perform 24 plain stitches, perform 12 stitches over the next 2, perform 24 plain stitches, skip 12 crosses, perform 24 plain stitches.

There are a total of thirty-six crosses.

Simple, with 3 additional trebles under each arm, and 6 extra over the 6 crosses at the center of the back.

There are forty crosses.

Simple, with an additional 6 in the rear.

There are forty-two crosses.

Similar to the 13th row.

There are forty-four crosses.

Similar to the 13th row.

There are forty-six crosses.

Simple, with no extra room in the back.

First, you will need to secure the end of the foundation chain, and then you will chain 5 to make spaces for the ribbon. After skipping two stitches, work a treble into the third-to-last stitch. This pattern is worked by chaining 2, skipping two stitches, and working one treble after each repetition.   Now, make a row of crosses around the garment, adding extra crosses at the edges to keep the work flat. When you're finished, the garment should look like this.   Continue by working a row of treble crochet stitches, gradually increasing the number of stitches at the edges to produce a smooth transition.

To complete the row, make a row of shells by working eight trebles into each stitch along the row.   The pattern is then completed as follows: skip three stitches, secure, then repeat the previous step. In the final step, you will construct an edge with the crochet silk by inserting a double crochet stitch in between the first two trebles of each shell. A double crochet should be worked in between the two treble stitches that are immediately following the chain 2 space.   Repeat the previous step a total of six times, each time beginning with a chain of two, then working two rounds of double crochet in the space between the shells, and ending with a chain of two.

Regarding the sleeves:

- Create 6 trebles below the arm and 36 over the 12 crosses.

- There are fourteen crosses.

- Simple, with 3 additional trebles under the arm, totaling 45.

- There are fifteen crosses.

- Just like the previous row, create 48 trebles.

- There are sixteen crosses.

- Just like the previous row, create 51 trebles.

- There are seventeen crosses.

- continuing with the same pattern, create 54 trebles in the next row.

Complete the process by incorporating shells and chain loops, following the instructions provided for the jacket's main section.   Thread one and one-fourth yards of ribbon through the neckline, then divide the remaining ribbon and thread it through the 7th row of the sleeve, creating a lovely bow on top.

Chapter 3
Bootees for kids

Procedure

Creating a pair of sensitive booties can be a thoughtful gesture that brings joy to both the baby and their mother.   Two adorable styles are offered, one in pink in color and white, perfect for adding a feminine grasp, and the other in blue along with white—blue being a popular choice for items for little boys.

- Starting with white Saxony, create a chain of 11 stitches, then turn.
- You can skip 1 stitch and then work a double crochet in each of the next 10 stitches. After that, turn in your work.
- Start by chaining 1, then work a double crochet in each of the next 10 stitches, making sure to work into the back loop to create a ribbed effect. Finally, turn in your work.

- Continue repeating the second row until you have a total of 8 ribs. At the end of the last row, chain 11, turn, skip 1 stitch, and work a double crochet in each of the next 10 stitches of the chain and in the next 10 double crochets. Chain 1, turn, and continue working to create 4 long ribs. Then, focusing only on the 10 double crochets, create 8 more short ribs. Finally, join the back of the leg to the foundation chain, making sure to incorporate each stitch.

Regarding the upper part of the leg:

- Create a chain of 3 stitches and proceed to make treble stitches all around, totaling 38 stitches. Join the stitches to the top of the initial chain of 3.
- Begin by pulling the stitch on the needle, then pull up a loop through the first and third stitches of the preceding row. Take up the yarn and draw it through the three loops on the needle simultaneously. Chain one to close the cluster. Repeat this process by drawing up a loop in the same place as the last one and another in the third stitch. Work off the loops as before and continue repeating this pattern around.
- Extend the stitch on the needle, create a loop in the area preceding the pineapple stitch from the previous row and another loop in the area following it. Complete the process as previously instructed, create a loop in the same area as before, another loop in the next area, and repeat the process.
- Similar to a 3D row, featuring a vibrant shade of blue.
- Just like a 3D row, but in white.
- Using a double stitch in every row, create a beautiful blue design.
- Begin by chaining 3 and then work a treble stitch into each double stitch. Finally, join the round.
- Using the color blue, create a double crochet stitch in the first stitch. Then, chain 3 and make another double crochet stitch in the same stitch. Skip the next stitch and repeat this pattern. Ensure a tidy finish.

Regarding the foot:

- Using a blue thread, create two stitches in each stitch around the bottom of the leg and instep.
- Two in each pair, occupying both strands of stitch to prevent a rib.
- Similar to the second row, but with a white color.
- Similar to the second row, but with a touch of blue.

Just like the second row, use white yarn and connect it to the previous row using a single crochet stitch on the opposite side.   Complete the project by adding a cord and tassels or ribbon, weaving them through the first row of trebles on the upper part of the leg.

Chapter 4
Child's Coat Sweater

Procedure

Here's a summary of the steps:

Front and Back Panels:

- Begin by making a chain of 160 stitches, then turn.

- Row 1: Work one double crochet in each stitch of the chain, chain 1, and turn.

- Row 2: Create a rib by working one double crochet in the back vein of each double crochet from the previous row.

- Row 3: Create star stitches along the rib. To make a star-stitch, chain 3, draw a loop through the 2nd and 3rd stitches of the chain (counting from the hook), and a loop through each of the two doubles. Yarn over and draw through all 5 loops on the hook, chain 1 to close the star, then draw a loop through the eye of the star you just made (under the 1 chain), another through the back part of the last perpendicular loop of the same star, and a loop through each of the two doubles. Close the star by working off all the loops, chain 1, and repeat this process to the end of the row. Turn.

- Keep switching within rib rows as well as rows of star stitches, making sure to work the star stitches on the right side. For the subsequent row, you'll want to cut the thread at the end of the next rib and fix it at the other end. The first row will obviously come out this way. After chaining 3, you can continue with the row.

- Once you've completed all four rows of star stitches as well as five rib rows, simply continue by working 39-star stitches on the next row, followed by adding a rib row.

- Keep going until you've got three sections of 39 stitches. Complete the row with double crochets, then cut and secure the yarn.

Putting things together:

To begin putting the sweater together, begin at the top of the front panel and leave the first six stitches, which should equal around three stars. Work your way down the panel. Repeat the star stitch pattern until the end of the row, at which point you should go on to the ribbing that was recommended. In each of the subsequent rounds, add two more rows of star stitches, alternating them with rows of rib stitches, and omitting one star at the top or neck-end of the piece.

Repeat similar procedures with the other half of the sweater front, making sure that it aligns with the piece that was completed previously. Connect the two portions at the middle of the back using a single crochet, making sure to carefully put the connect through a loop of each section to create a join that is both flawless and undetectable. Make armholes by cutting apertures for the arms into the garment.

Edging:

Begin by crocheting 10 rows of double crochet within the entire garment, including the fronts, bottom, and neck. When creating mitered corners, remember to gradually increase the width at the lower corners with each row.

Buttonholes:

Start by chaining 5, skipping 5 stitches, and continuing this technique until you have openings in the fifth row that are uniformly spaced apart. This will allow you to construct buttonholes on the front of the garment. Make sure that you do a double crochet stitch in each of the stitches that make up the 5-chain buttonhole as you work backward on the next row.

To begin the sleeves, chain 80 stitches, including one turning chain. This will be your starting point. On top of the chain, work a row of double crochet stitches, then work 40 star stitches in the space left over. Continue working until you have completed 10 rows of the star stitches and 11 rows of the rib stitches, making sure that the star stitches are always worked on the right side.   By using a single crochet and repeating the procedures used for the back of the garment, you can join the sleeve seam on the opposite side.

To complete the project, work 12 rounds of double crochet, being careful to work one double crochet into each stitch and turning back after each round. Turning back after each round is an essential step in this technique.

Final Steps:

- Sew the sleeves into the armholes.
- Sew buttons onto the sweater, corresponding to the buttonholes on the front.

You can adjust the size of this sweater by starting with a longer initial chain and adding more rows of star stitches and ribs to maintain the proportions. The combination of stitches creates an attractive design for the sweater.

7: INTRODUCTION OF THE ART OF AMIGURUMI

Scarves are a common first project for someone learning to crochet since, well, they are just long rectangles! But you can make your own little sculptures after you get more proficient with your crochet hook and feel ready to tackle more difficult jobs. You can create adorable and enjoyable plush toys by utilizing the amigurumi techniques.

Chapter 1
what is Amigurumi?

Definition and Meaning

The term "amigurumi" combines two Japanese words: "nuigurumi," which means stuffed doll, and "ami," which means knitted or crocheted. Though they can be made in any size, these stuffed animals are often made with lightweight yarns and are modest in size. Amigurumi has become a popular art form all around the world, and there is a burgeoning community of crafters who produce, exchange and market their original designs.

Brief History

There exist records of dolls made by knitting and crocheting from the Shang period in China, which leads some historians to believe that this art form originated there. With the interactions between China and Japan from the beginning of the 17th century, during the Edo period, the craft began to gain popularity in Japan.

The 1970s saw the debut of the first real amigurumi dolls. The idea emerged in tandem with other kawaii (cute) fads, such as chibis, which are "little" representations of everyday items and people, and early (though not prototypical) forms of manga and animation.

Chapter 2
Distinguishing Crochet from Amigurumi

How Crochet is different from amigurumi?

You can use knitting or crocheting to make amigurumi, which is the finished stuffed animal or doll. The finished product, called an amigurumi, can be made through crocheting. Numerous other techniques can be used in crocheting to produce a variety of items, such as blankets, clothes, hats, socks, scarves, and many other items. To put it simply:

"Crochet is basically the method of creation"

"Amigurumi is an outcome"

Chapter 3
Key Features of Amigurumi

Amigurumi is a unique crochet style that showcases small, stuffed, and irresistibly cute characters and creatures.

Characteristics

Notable characteristics of amigurumi encompass:

- Compact Creations: Amigurumi specializes in crafting small and adorable items like stuffed animals, dolls, and miniature characters. These items are frequently small enough to fit in the palm of your hand, making them ideal for collectors or as decorative pieces.

- Adorableness: Amigurumi designs frequently center around crafting lovable and charming characters. The facial features, characterized by their captivating eyes and petite mouths, enhance their charm.

- Round Shape: Numerous amigurumi projects employ single crochet stitches worked in a continuous spiral. This method produces a smooth and uniform form, perfect for crafting the body and head of the amigurumi character.

- Filling: Amigurumi items are usually filled with fiberfill or other materials to create a soft and plush texture. The stuffing is carefully incorporated to achieve the desired shape and volume.

- Limited Movement: Amigurumi characters typically have limited ability to move. While some may have movable arms or legs, many are designed to be stationary decorative items.

- A wide array of designs are available in the world of Amigurumi, ranging from adorable animals to fantastical creatures, human-like characters, delectable food items, and much more. The potential for creativity in amigurumi knows no bounds.

- 9. Amigurumi can be enjoyed by crocheters of all skill levels. Novice crafters can begin their amigurumi journey with straightforward patterns and gradually challenge themselves with more intricate designs as they become more skilled.

- 10. Thoughtful presents and cherished items: Amigurumi creations are frequently crafted as heartfelt gifts for dear ones or treasured by passionate collectors. They possess a distinct allure that renders them perfect for noteworthy events or cherished mementos.

- 12. Community and Sharing: Amigurumi has a passionate and supportive community of crafters who love to share their creations, patterns, and tips with others. Many people in the amigurumi community use social media platforms and online forums to connect with like-minded individuals.

The charm of amigurumi lies in its petite size, adorable designs, and endless possibilities to bring various characters and creatures to life through crochet. It provides a one-of-a-kind and delightful avenue for crafters to showcase their artistic flair and create lovely, handcrafted pieces.

Chapter 4
Some Step-by-Step Amigurumi Creations

If you are interested in mastering the art of creating intricate crochet designs, this section is perfect for you!

Kitten Amigurumis

Steps

- Begin by making a magic ring with yarn.
- Use a single stitch in the ring to construct the body.
- Keep crocheting a tail, ears as well head in separate stitches.
- After sewing the parts together, fill them with fiberfill.
- Attached are any required ornaments and embroider the facial details.

Supplies

Yarn, safety eyes (optional), fiberfill, crochet hook, and embroidery thread

Pattern

Work 6 single crochet stitches into a magic ring starting at the outside of the ring. Each stitch has an increase (12 stitches). 18 stitches total—1 single crochet and 1 increase. 24 stitches total—2 single crochets and 1 increase. Work in rounds of crocheting until the desired length is achieved. Stitch the head onto the body and insert fiberfill inside. If desired, add safety eyes and embroider the facial features.

Dinosaur Amigurumi

Steps

- Work the body in single crochet stitches, starting with a magic ring.
- Make the tail, legs, and head in separate pieces.
- Stuff the parts and assemble them.
- Utilizing felt or stitching, add eyeballs, spikes, and other embellishments.

Supplies

Yarn, safety eyes (optional), fiberfill, crochet hook, and embroidery thread

Pattern

Work 6 single crochet stitches into a magic ring starting at the outside of the ring. Each stitch has an increase (12 stitches). 18 stitches total—1 single crochet and 1 increase. 24 stitches total—2 single crochets and 1 increase. Work in rounds of crocheting until the desired length is achieved. After sewing the parts together, fill them with fiberfill. Make use of felt or embroidery to add eyes, spikes, and other details.

Crafted plush unicorns

Steps

- Work in single crochet stitches in a magic ring to begin the body.
- Work each ear, horn, and skull separately in crochet.
- Stitch the parts together and insert fiberfill.
- Sew on the nose, eyes, and any other required features.

Supplies

Yarn, safety eyes (optional), fiberfill, crochet hook, and embroidery thread

Pattern

Work 6 single crochet stitches into a magic ring starting at the outside of the ring. Each stitch has an increase (12 stitches). 18 stitches total—1 single crochet and 1 increase. 24 stitches total—2 single crochets and 1 increase. Work in rounds of crocheting until the desired length is achieved. After sewing the parts together, fill them with fiberfill. Sew on the nose, eyes, and any other desirable features.

Must try these to enjoy amigurumi creations!

Chapter 5
Fun and Easy Amigurumi Projects

These five kid-friendly amigurumi projects are simple and entertaining:

Little Cupcake

Materials

Yarn, safety eyes (optional), fiberfill, crochet hook, and embroidery thread

Pattern

Work 6 single crochet stitches into a magic ring starting at the outside of the ring. Each stitch has an increase (12 stitches). 18 stitches total—1 single crochet and 1 increase. Work in rounds of crocheting until the desired height is achieved. Close the bottom with a stitch and fill with fiberfill. Top with a cherry sewn with embroidery thread.

Tiny Turtle

Materials

Yarn, safety eyes (optional), fiberfill, crochet hook, and embroidery thread

Pattern

Work 6 single crochet stitches into a magic ring starting at the outside of the ring. Each stitch has an increase (12 stitches). 18 stitches total—1 single crochet and 1 increase. Work in rounds of crocheting until the desired size is reached. After sewing the parts together, fill them with fiberfill. Sew on the eyes and attach a small shell to the rear.

Little Ladybug

Supplies

Yarn, safety eyes (optional), fiberfill, crochet hook, and embroidery thread

Pattern

Work 6 single crochet stitches into a magic ring starting at the outside of the ring. Each stitch has an increase (12 stitches). 18 stitches total—1 single crochet and 1 increase. Work in rounds of crocheting until the desired size is reached. After sewing the parts together, fill them with fiberfill. Stitch the eyes, and give the crimson body some black dots.

Little Octopus

Supplies

Yarn, fiberfill, crochet hook, embroidery thread, and (optional) safety eyes

Pattern

Work 6 single crochet stitches into a magic ring starting at the outside of the ring. Each stitch has an increase (12 stitches). Work in rounds of crocheting until the desired length is achieved. After sewing the parts together, fill them with fiberfill. Use embroidery thread to add little tentacles and embroidered eyeballs.

Little Bunny

Supplies

Yarn, safety eyes (optional), fiberfill, crochet hook, and embroidery thread

Pattern

Work 6 single crochet stitches into a magic ring starting at the outside of the ring. Each stitch has an increase (12 stitches). 18 stitches total—1 single crochet and 1 increase. Work in rounds of crocheting until the desired size is reached. After sewing the parts together, fill them with fiberfill. Sew on the nose, eyes, and droopy ears.

Enjoy creating these sweet amigurumi!

8: AFGHAN TO TUNISIAN: AN OVERVIEW OF DIFFERENT CROCHET TECHNIQUES

Chapter 1
Different Crochet Techniques

Crocheting comes in a plethora of forms. I adore crocheting for yet another reason. There are a plethora of options and ways available for exploration. It would take a long time to list every kind of crochet, though. I will thus provide you with a list of the most common sorts that I have encountered.

Many of these crochet patterns are made up of their own special stitches, but some are just variations of standard crochet patterns. As much as I appreciate learning about them all, I hope you do too!

Afghan Crochet

Also called Tunisian crochet, this technique uses a long crochet hook and a special stitching pattern to create a cloth that looks like it was knitted.

Aran Crochet

This crocheting technique is reminiscent of classic Aran knitting designs, with its textured stitches and elaborate cable patterns.

Bavarian Crochet

Bavarian crochet is a technique that produces a visually arresting and textured cloth by using geometric designs and colorful yarn.

Bullion Crochet

Bullion stitches are a kind of crocheting in which the hook is wrapped around several times before being pulled through the loop, giving the impression of being raised and coiled.

Broomstick Lace Crochet

This type of crocheting entails looping yarn around a broomstick or large knitting needle to produce openwork lace patterns.

Bruges Lace Crochet

The method of "Bruges Lace Crochet" involves using crocheted ribbons or strips to create intricate and beautiful designs.

Clothesline crochet

This technique is used to make strong, useful objects like baskets and mats by crocheting around a cord or clothesline.

Clones Lace Crochet

Clones lace is an elaborate crocheting technique from Ireland that frequently incorporates three-dimensional components such as leaves and flowers.

Filet Crochet

Filet crochet is a technique that uses filled and open squares to create patterns or images inside fabric. It is frequently utilized for ornamental items like curtains and tablecloths.

Finger crocheting

This method uses your fingertips to manipulate the yarn and make crochet stitches instead of a crochet hook.

Freeform Crochet

This creative and artistic method of crocheting does not adhere to rigid guidelines or patterns. It permits artistic expression in the creation of distinctive, organic forms.

Hairpin Lace Crochet

This crochet technique uses a hairpin lace loom to produce fabric strips with eye-catching loops and lacy patterns.

Micro crocheting

Micro crocheting is the technique of creating tiny objects and minute features by using incredibly fine yarn and tiny hooks.

Overlay Crochet

This technique creates intricate and textured designs by combining several layers of crocheted cloth.

Pineapple Crochet

Pineapple crochet patterns are used to make shawls and doilies, among other beautiful items. They frequently have elaborate, pineapple-like embellishments.

Tunisian crochet

As previously noted, Tunisian crochet, also called Afghan crochet, is a crochet technique that blends knitting and crochet techniques to produce a distinctive fabric. It is worked with a long hook.

With their own qualities and uses, each of these crochet techniques offers a plethora of imaginative opportunities for crocheters.

Chapter 2
How to Bavarian Crochet?

Are you prepared to master a brand-new stitch combination that produces vibrant crochet squares? Introducing Bavarian crochet Bavarian crochet is made with interlocking rounds that start with a cross shape in the middle and blend together to create gradients and use up leftover yarn.

Though it resembles Catherine's Wheel, this basic technique is relatively new and differs in how the rounds join. As your work develops, you might even start to feel like you are in a granny square.

As they do use a lot of yarn, this stitch and projects made with it are sometimes referred to as yarn eaters. It is common to see Bavarian crocheting work in multiple colors because that can be a great way to work through your stash. However, even when only one color is used, the texture is still lovely.

This chapter will teach you how to work Bavarian crochet in its most basic square form. This section will teach you how to work Bavarian crochet in its basic square form.

What you'll need?

- Simple yarn in a variety of hues
- Hook
- scissors
- Yarn needle

Method

Phase One

Step 1 of Round 1: Crochet a Beginning Ring

Setup for Round 1: Chain 6 and slip stitch into a ring.

Step 2 of Round 1: Begin the First Spoke Chain 5.

Wrap the yarn tail over the yarn that is being worked with each chain as you begin to save time when weaving in the ends. You can begin each new color by doing this.

Step 3 of Round 1: Create a Triple Crochet Cluster

Work 4 treble crochets to make a treble crochet cluster.

Before you yarn over and draw the last loop through every stitch, you should have five loops on the hook.

Step 4 of Round 1:

Single crochet into the beginning ring after finishing the First Spoke Chain 5

Step 5 of Round 1: Repeat to Finish the Round

To get four spokes in total, repeat this round's steps two through five three times.

Slip stitches the round to join it.

Phase Two

Step 1 of Round 2: Work around the First Spoke

Stage 2 setup: Single crochet into first round single crochet after chain one.

Sequence 2

For treble crochet, yarn over twice. Put the hook through the top of the treble crocheted four times from the first round. This is the "eye" that was made when the loop was drawn through each stitch. In the following step, finish this stitch.

Step Two of Round 1: Double Crochet within the Spoke

Chain 1, treble crochet 4, etc

The treble crochet that was started in the step prior is included in this.

Chain 1, treble crochet 4, and treble crochet 4.

Step 3 of Round 2: Anchor the Stitches

Add a single crochet to the single crochet that was worked in the round before. The shell's shape is now guaranteed.

Step 4 of Round 2: Repeat to Finish the Round

Add a shell shape to each spoke by repeating steps two and three.

End the yarn and slip stitch the round to join. This is a great time for weaving at the end of the initial color to save time later.

Step 1 of Round 3: Begin a New Yarn Color

Stage 3 setup: Join new color yarn with single crochet, working into the first chain-1 space from the previous round.

In Round 3, Step 2, create a Back Post Treble Crochet Cluster by yarn over twice.

To begin a back post treble crochet, insert your hook so that it passes in front of the subsequent treble crocheting from the previous round.

Together, treble crochet four back posts. Before creating a loop through all of the loops on the hook and finishing the stitch, there should be five loops on it.

Round 3, Step 3: Single crochet within the chain-1 space created in the previous round and finish the Corner Chain 5.

Create a Back Post Treble Crochet Cluster in Round 3, Step 4.

Triple crochet 8 together in the back post. By the time you draw a loop through the last one and finish the stitch, there should be nine loops on the hook.

Round 3, Step 5: Single crochet into the chain-1 space created in the previous round and finish the Side Chain 5.

Step 6 of Round 3: Repeat to Finish the Round

Steps one through five should be repeated, adding to each nook and side starting with chain 5. Slip stitch the round to join it.

Round 4, Step 1: Around the Corner Treble Crochet

Setup for Round 4: Chain 1 and single crochet into the round before single crochet.

Working into the previous round's "eye" of the cluster, treble crochet 4, chain 1 twice, and then treble crochet 4.

In the single crocheting from the previous round, single crochet.

Step 2 of Round 4: Triple Crochet the Side

Working into the previous round's "eye" of the cluster, chain 1, treble crochet 4, and treble crochet 4 in the single crocheting from the previous round, single crochet.

Step 3 of Round 4: Repeat to Finish the Round

Steps one and two should be repeated, adding to each corner and side (beginning at the first treble crochet).

To get the size square you want, repeat rounds three and four as many times as necessary. As the piece grows, you will simply add more side stitch repeats since all the corners are the same.

The beauty of the Bavarian stitch is truly highlighted when the colors are added in a rainbow order or in a gradient of a single hue (for instance, working from pink to red to burgundy).

9: WHAT SHOULD EVERY BEGINNERS KNOW AND FAQs

Chapter 1
What should every beginner know?

All crocheters will concur that having the proper tools improves abilities and imagination. Having quality tools on hand is crucial and should be carefully picked, regardless of your level of experience or desire to master new methods. Though they are quite different yarn crafts, knitting and crocheting share a lot of similarities few necessary types of equipment are shared by each of these crafts. Therefore, if you already knit, you may already have the accessories in your collection. If you are just starting out with crochet, here are some fundamental things you need to understand:

Supplies for Crochet

You will need a crochet hook, yarn, scissors, stitch markers, and a tapestry needle to get started with crocheting. A tapestry needle is also recommended.

Choosing the Right Yarn

Having confidence in your ability to select the appropriate yarn for your project is essential. It is important to take into consideration the yarn's weight, texture, and color.

Choices Available in Crochet Hooks

 Hooks for crocheting are available in a variety of sizes and materials. You need to select the appropriate size hook for the yarn that you have.

Stitches for Crochet

In addition to the single, double and half-double crochet stitches, there exist numerous other types of crochet stitches. To get started with crochet, it is important that you learn the fundamental stitches first.

Patterns for Crochet

A crochet pattern is a set of instructions for constructing a specific type of object. You ought to get started with easy patterns and work your way up to more difficult ones as time goes on.

Control of Tension

Maintaining even and consistent tension during the stitching process is essential. In order to improve your crocheting skills, you should get some practice managing the tension in your stitches.

How to Read Crochet Charts?

Crochet charts, also known as crochet diagrams, are visual representations of crochet patterns. If you want to increase your crocheting abilities, you need to learn how to interpret crochet charts.

If you have a firm grasp of these fundamentals, you will be well on your way to becoming a crochet pro and producing stunning works of art.

Chapter 2
General Questions

General Questions about Crochet

Is crocheting a difficult skill to learn?

Learning to crochet is really not that hard! The good news is that all you really need to know are around five fundamental stitches.

These stitches (chain, single, double, treble, and slip) can be used to create any of the beautiful patterns you have seen, including toys, blankets, doilies, and more.

Furthermore, it does not really matter if you start with crocheting or knitting first. When you first start out, both have a steep learning curve, but you will enjoy every minute as soon as you get the hang of making the stitches.

Who invented crochet?

The origin of crochet cannot be traced to a single individual. Historians differ as to where it all began: some point to 1500s Italy, some to ancient Persia, and still others to South America. Whatever its origin, crochet really developed from a variety of crafts, including knitting, embroidery, and tapestry, and it still does.

Which Is Faster: Knitting or Crocheting?

Crocheting is often faster, but it also depends on the person and the task. Knitting is a time-consuming hobby that demands a great deal of patience, especially when creating intricate items like sweaters. It also takes longer to build up knitting stitches because they are often smaller than crochet ones. However, compared to knitting crafts, crochet projects typically require more yarn. Thus, intricate tasks requiring a large amount of yarn may require more time than a similar knitted one.

Describe amigurumi.

The term "crocheted or knitted soft toy," or "amigurumi" in Japanese, refers to a class of toys that are primarily made of crochet and have become quite popular on the internet. Amitirami toys, also known as amis, are available in many sizes and forms and can be customized to your preference.

Chapter 3
Questions about the supplies, materials, and accessories

The following are some commonly asked questions (FAQs) concerning materials, accessories, and supplies for crocheting:

What essential materials are required to begin crocheting?

To begin, you will need yarn, crochet hooks, and scissors. Additionally useful are stitch markers and a yarn needle.

What is the best way to select yarn for a project?

Yarn is available in various weights (thickness) and fiber kinds (such as wool, acrylic, and cotton). The weight of the yarn should be as suggested by the pattern; the type of fiber to use will depend on your own taste and the intended use of the creation.

What is the use of a tapestry or yarn needle in crocheting?

Yarn needles are used to finish your crochet items neatly by sewing sections together, and weaving in loose ends.

Is a crochet gauge tool necessary?

To ensure precise sizing, use a crochet gauge tool, such as a ruler with marked measures, to make sure your stitches fit the gauge of the design.

What distinguishes straight from circular crochet hooks?

A flexible cable runs between the hook and the handle of circular crochet hooks. They are employed for huge, flat objects such as blankets, or for projects made in the round. Traditional straight hooks work better for smaller, flat objects.

What is the purpose of blocking mats and pins in crochet?

Your completed crochet pieces can be shaped and set to the desired size and form using blocking mats and pins. This is particularly useful for delicate projects like lace.

Are left-handed crocheters able to use specific tools?

Although left-handed crocheters can use regular crochet hooks, left-handed crafters can also use hooks made especially for them. The ergonomic design of these hooks allows for left-handed techniques.

Which accessories are optional for experienced crocheters?

Stitch counters, advanced stitch markers, and specialty hooks for particular methods, such as Tunisian crochet, are items that experienced crocheters may want to take into consideration.

Can I use everyday objects as crocheting tools?

Yes, in a pinch, a lot of commonplace objects like hairpins, paperclips, and pencils can double as temporary crochet hooks or stitch markers.

Remember that the choice of supplies and accessories can vary depending on your crochet style and preferences, so don't hesitate to experiment and find what works best for you.

Chapter 4
Glossary

Afghan needlework

Watch the Tunisian stitch. Afghan stitches have a vertical bar on top and are fashioned like tiny squares with two horizontal yarn strands.

Amidaguzami

a knitting or crocheting technique used in Japan to create little creatures and other items, frequently with human traits.

Afghan square

Another term for the granny square

Blocking

Adjusting the completed piece's shape by either steam-pressing it after it has been pinned out or soaking it and pinning it out

Chain loop, chain space

A space in the cloth is created by working a length of chain stitches in between basic stitches.

Decrease

Taking off a stitch or stitches to shape the fabric and decrease the amount of working stitches

Dye lot

a note made while the yarn is being dyed in order to identify it. For each project, use yarn from a single dye lot; do not combine dye batches to avoid tone changes in your crocheted cloth.

Fibers

Yarn is composed of fibers, which can be from plants, animals, or man-made (synthetic) materials. After processing, the fibers are spun into yarn.

Front and rear posts

Parts of a crochet stitch that are vertical.

Foundation chain

The chain stitch foundation on which the first row of crochet is constructed

Gauge

The amount of stitches and rows in a specific area, which is typically a 4 in (10 cm) square. Furthermore, the crocheter's relative tightness. Correct gauges can be achieved by adjusting the hook size.

Increase

Increasing the number of working stitches and shaping the fabric by adding a stitch or stitches

Row

Make a piece of crocheted cloth by going back and forth in rows At the end of each row, turn the work to form a turning chain, and begin working across the next row again.

Stitch marker

An apparatus for labeling positions on a work in progress is frequently used to indicate the beginning and finish of a round in circular crochet.

Sphere-winder

a machine that is used to wind yarn hanks into balls and to wind two or more strands together to create double-stranded yarn Frequently combined with a quick.

Tension

A different word for gauge

Yarn

Spun fibers that form a lengthy strand Natural fibers, synthetic fibers, a combination of the two, or even unconventional materials can be used to create yarns.

10: CROCHET BUSINESS

Chapter 1
Transforming Your Crochet Hobby into Profit

Many people find crocheting to be a creative and calming pastime. But for those who have perfected their crocheting and want to advance their art, it is feasible to make their hobby a successful business. Making money from your crochet hobby requires careful planning and a few important procedures.

Maximizing the Profitability of Your Crochet Designs

This topic focuses on realizing the possibility of making money from your crochet pastime. It entails realizing the worth of your handcrafted crochet goods and exploring revenue streams for them.

Selling Handmade Crochet Products: Revenue Path

This section probably explores the more practical side of selling your crochet crafts, such as pricing your goods, putting up an internet store, and handling customer service. It all comes down to knowing how to turn sales into money.

Examining Market Potential for Your Craft

Conducting market research is essential to determining the potential and level of demand for the crochet goods you produce. This may include looking into different internet marketplaces, craft fairs, or regional markets where you can sell and exhibit your products.

Promoting Your Crochet Works: The Influence of Cricut Designs

To draw in new clients, marketing is crucial. This topic might include how using Cricut designs and technology—whether it be for labels, tags, or packaging—can improve the way your crochet items are presented and marketed.

Finding Successful Cricut Businesses

This might look into starting a business that goes along with your crocheting, like selling labels that can be personalized, packaging supplies, or other Cricut-designed goods that you can sell with your crochet creations.

Making Money Off of Your Finished Crochet Items:

Crochet goods can be directly sold, but there are other ways to generate income. This subject might cover different ways to make money, like giving crochet lessons, creating patterns, or working with other creatives and companies.

Essentially, these subjects are about learning how to turn your artistic abilities into a profitable venture by investigating different channels for product sales, advertising, and business growth. They also involve making lovely crochet items.

Chapter 2
Pricing Your Craft with Precision

Setting the right price for your handmade crafts is a critical aspect of turning your creative passion into a sustainable business. It involves understanding the true value of your work and making informed pricing decisions.

Valuing Your Creative Work

Before setting prices, recognize the worth of your creative labor. Consider the time, skill, and artistic expression that go into each piece. Remember that customers appreciate and are willing to pay for unique, handcrafted items.

Navigating Requests: How to Handle Crafting Commissions:

Handling custom crafting requests can be a profitable avenue. Ensure that you charge adequately for custom work, considering the additional time, materials, and effort required to meet specific customer needs.

Calculating Costs:

Your Time, Expertise, and Materials: Calculate the actual costs associated with each craft. This includes the cost of materials, your time and expertise, and any overhead expenses. Accurately tracking costs is essential for setting sustainable prices.

Pricing Considerations:

Project Complexity, Size, and Delivery: Consider the complexity and size of each project when determining the price. Larger or more intricate pieces typically require higher prices. Delivery costs, if applicable, should also be factored in.

Originality vs. Repetition:

Making Smart Business Decisions: Original, one-of-a-kind pieces can often command higher prices. However, if you plan to produce multiples of a design, decide on a fair pricing structure that accounts for your time and materials.

Deliverables, Locations, and Project Durations:

Take into account the type of deliverables (e.g., digital files, physical items), your location (local or international market), and the time it takes to complete a project. These factors can influence your pricing strategy.

Establishing Your Minimum Pricing Standards:

Set a minimum pricing standard to ensure that your business remains profitable and sustainable. This minimum should consider your base costs and the income you need to cover your time and effort adequately.

In summary, pricing your craft accurately is a crucial aspect of turning your creative passion into a successful business. Recognize the value of your work, account for all costs, and consider various factors when determining prices. By doing so, you can ensure that your craft not only brings you joy but also financial reward.

Chapter 3
Craft Your Creative Business

Starting a creative business, especially in crochet, involves several key steps that can help you turn your passion into a successful entrepreneurial journey.

Launching Your Entrepreneurial Journey:

Begin by establishing your business identity, registering your craft business, and setting clear goals. A well-thought-out business plan will serve as your roadmap for success.

Targeting the Right Client:

Identify your ideal customer. Understand their preferences, needs, and buying behaviors. Tailor your crochet items to appeal to this specific target audience.

Local Markets:

A Stepping Stone to Success: Participating in local craft markets, fairs, and events can be an excellent way to gain exposure, build a customer base, and refine your sales skills. These markets provide a stepping stone for success.

The Digital Frontier:

Selling Your Crochet Online: Embrace the digital age by selling your crochet items online. Create an e-commerce website or open a shop on popular platforms like Etsy. This enables you to reach a global audience and expand your sales opportunities.

Crafting a Successful Online Presence:

Social Media Marketing: Leverage the power of social media to market your crochet business. Create engaging and visually appealing content on platforms like Instagram, Facebook, and Pinterest. Interact with your audience, build a following, and drive traffic to your online store.

In crafting your creative business, a combination of local and online strategies can pave the way for a successful venture. Remember to stay true to your craft, connect with your customers, and adapt to the changing business landscape for long-term success.

Chapter 4
Becoming a Professional Cricut Designer

Transitioning into a professional Cricut designer involves a series of crucial steps and attributes to excel in this creative field.

Unleashing Your Unique Creativity:

As a Cricut designer, your creativity is your greatest asset. Unleash your imagination to create designs that stand out and capture attention. Find your unique style and let it shine through your work.

Focusing Your Craft and Expertise:

Specialization is key. Focus on specific areas within Cricut design, such as creating SVG files, crafting custom designs, or producing patterns for various projects. Specialization can set you apart in a competitive market.

Consistency as a Key to Success:

Consistency in quality and output is essential. Maintain a steady work pace and produce designs of the highest standard. This builds trust with clients and customers.

Perseverance and the Art of Tenacity:

Expect challenges and setbacks on your journey. Perseverance and tenacity are your allies. Keep pushing forward, learning from failures, and adapting to changing trends.

Lifelong Learning: The Path to Mastery:

The design field is ever-evolving. Keep learning and improving your skills. Stay updated on the latest Cricut technologies, design software, and market trends to remain competitive.

Quality Control: Building Your Brand Reputation:

Your brand reputation depends on the quality of your work. Implement rigorous quality control processes to ensure your designs meet or exceed expectations. A solid reputation can lead to long-term success.

Becoming a professional Cricut designer is not just about creating visually appealing designs but also about mastering your craft, building a strong brand, and persistently pursuing excellence in a dynamic and creative field.

Conclusion

As we reach the conclusion of this crochet ebook, I sincerely hope that you have experienced the immense joy and fulfillment that this timeless craft has to offer. Crochet goes beyond the simple act of looping yarn; it serves as a means of artistic expression, a source of relaxation, and a catalyst for creativity. It is a skill that brings people together, enables the creation of unique and meaningful items, and instills a feeling of pride with each stitch.

You have mastered the essential stitches, techniques, and patterns, but your crochet adventure does not have to end just yet. It is a craft that is always changing, and you now have the ability to delve into more complex projects, create your own designs, and play around with different types of yarn, textures, and colors.

Whether you are crafting cozy coverings, fashion-forward supplies, delicate lacework, or amusing amigurumi, crochet allows you to add a personal touch to your creations and showcase your individual style and personality.

So, stay engaged and let your imagination run wild. Spread your passion for crochet to your loved ones and, in the future, continue this craft with the next generation. Keep seeking inspiration from the beauty of nature, art, and the world around you, and let it flow into your crochet projects.

The world of crochet is incredibly expansive, offering a multitude of patterns, ideas, and techniques just waiting to be discovered. Always keep in mind that in the world of crochet, every misstep is a chance for personal growth and improvement. Be bold, unleash your creativity, and wholeheartedly embrace the unique quirks that give your projects their distinctiveness.

Thank you for joining us on this crochet adventure. May your future be filled with endless hours of crochet bliss, and may the beautiful creations you make bring warmth, comfort, and joy to both yourself and your loved ones. Crochet is not just a craft; it is a labor of love, a work of art, and a never-ending source of inspiration. Continue your crochet projects and keep unleashing your creativity.

Made in United States
Troutdale, OR
12/26/2023

16422154R00084